CULTURAL
SHAKESPEARE

Essays in the Shakespeare myth

CULTURAL SHAKESPEARE

Essays in the Shakespeare myth

GRAHAM HOLDERNESS

UNIVERSITY OF HERTFORDSHIRE PRESS

First published in Great Britain in 2001 by
University of Hertfordshire Press
Learning and Information Services
University of Hertfordshire
College Lane
Hatfield
Hertfordshire AL10 9AB

A catalogue record for this book is available from the British Library.

ISBN 1 902806 11 5 paperback
ISBN 1 902806 14 x casebound

Design by Geoff Green, Cambridge CB4 5RA.
Cover design by John Robertshaw, Harpenden AL5 2TB
Printed in Great Britain by J. W. Arrowsmith Ltd.

In memory of Francis Barker
1952–1999
λαλει και μη σιωπησησ

Acknowledgements

·ᴥ·

I AM GRATEFUL TO Manchester University Press for permission to reprint as Chapter 6 'Shakespeare's England: Britain's Shakespeare', from *Shakespeare and National Culture*, edited by John Joughin (Manchester: Manchester University Press (1997), pp. 19–41; and to Taylor and Francis for permission to reprint '"What ish my nation?": Shakespeare and National Identities', *Textual Practice*, 5/1 (1991), pp. 80–99, and 'Shakespeare and Heritage', *Textual Practice* 6/2 (1992), pp. 247–63, as Chapters 4 and 5. Thanks are also due to editors John Joughin and Alan Sinfield. Chapters 6 and 7 are here published by kind permission of my co-authors Andrew Murphy and Bryan Loughrey.

Contents

ॐ

Preface

۶۹

THE TWO TERMS of this book's title – 'culture' and 'myth' – map the territory of its contents, which span more or less a decade of work (1984–94) in a particular area of Shakespeare studies. The sub-title derives from a collection of essays by various hands, published in 1988 as *The Shakespeare Myth*. The term 'myth' was derived from Roland Barthes' *Mythologies[i]*. It was an attempt to identify a powerful cultural institution, constructed around the figure of Shakespeare, that could be analysed to some degree separately from the person of the Elizabethan dramatist, and the texts of his works.

Traditional Shakespeare criticism, as it is still very widely practised, consists of reading and interpreting the plays and poems; seeking to unlock their intrinsic meanings by reference to the author's assumed 'intentions' or to the historical context in which he wrote; analysing the plays in relation to their origins in the Elizabethan theatre and so on. *The Shakespeare Myth* sought a different approach:

> It is incumbent (I said in the Preface) upon a new critical intervention into the Shakespeare debate to … break from the conventions of textual re-reading, and to address directly those fields of discourse and those institutional practices in which the cultural phenomenon of Shakespeare operates with some form of signifying power. The contributors to this volume were encouraged to

look behind and beyond the 'plays' as commonly constituted and presented, the narrowly defined forms of literary text, historical phenomenon and theatrical production, and to recognise 'Shakespeare' wherever and whenever that authorial construction is manifested, in forms as diverse as television advertisements, comedy sketches, Stratford-upon-Avon tourist attractions, the design on a twenty pound note or a narcissistic portrait in a homoerotic 'physique' magazine'[ii].

Or as Terry Eagleton put it in his 'Afterword', the book was a study of 'Shakespeare', rather than of Shakespeare (p. 204), a name which, Eagleton went on to suggest, 'is merely metonymic of an entire cultural-political formation, and thus more akin to "Disney" or "Rockefeller" than to "Jane Smith"' (204).

'Shakespeare' was seen throughout *The Shakespeare Myth* as a site of cultural production, a ground for the making of social meaning or as an ideological apparatus at work in contemporary culture. The focus of the study was therefore not, as in more traditional criticism, on the great dramatist who formulated, in memorable works, eternal truths; but rather on the various ways in which 'Shakespeare' has been made to mean different things in different historical and cultural contexts. The method of the book was thus more a kind of sociology or politics of cultural history than anything that could be recognised as literary criticism[iii]. We were looking at the plays not as artifacts or as writings produced within a particular historical formation but at the uses to which they have been put within the framework of the 'Shakespeare' institution. Hence the book was structured into two parts. The first dealt with 'Discursive Formations' and examined the Shakespeare myth at work in such general social experiences as the tourist industry of Stratford-upon-Avon (reflected here in the essay on 'Bardolatry'), the political conflicts surrounding the Globe reconstruction project and how Shakespeare's presence is felt in popular culture and in contemporary sexual politics. The second was addressed to the 'Cultural Practices' of reproducing Shakespeare in theatre, education and television.

The title obviously caught on. James Wood in *The Guardian* referred to 'a Shakespeare Myth school of criticism' (2 April 1992, p. 26). At least one book, *Appropriating Shakespeare*, picked up the phrase in its sub-title: *'the works and the myth'*[iv]. More surprisingly, considering the vast growth in this kind of criticism since the book's publication, it still seems to serve as a useful catch phrase. On the World Wide Web can be found the syllabus of a course, taught at Wesleyan University in America, entitled 'The Shakespeare Myth' which is described as focusing on:

> Shakespeare as a site of cultural production, as one of the places where our society's understanding of itself is worked out.

The course examines how the Shakespeare corpus is continually reproduced in edited texts and theatrical adaptations; how Shakespeare's reputation as 'genius' and 'national poet' developed in the course of the eighteenth century; how Shakespeare functions, as drama and literature, in different cultural situations, including those of America and Britain and how the plays are reproduced in (often radically innovative) modern film versions. Barbara Hodgdon sums up this general acceptance of the term in her 1998 book *The Shakespeare Trade:*

> The ideological contours of the historically determined 'Shakespeare Myth' and how it functions to sustain cultural consensus has by now become a commonplace of cultural criticism[v].

Here the fact that the term 'cultural criticism' can be regarded as so commonplace that it contains it own commonplaces, is an indication of the deep and large-scale changes that have taken place in the discipline of literary criticism since the early 1970s. Then, the impact of intellectual movements such as post-structuralism, marxism, feminism and post-colonialism were beginning to filter into the academy and to generate a recognisably 'radical' criticism. Such criticism has now become mainstream and although it has lost much of the political urgency it possessed in those days when literary criticism could be seen as part of a socialist critique of contemporary capitalist ideology and society, it has certainly changed the relations between theory and practice in what people actually do when they study 'English'.

In *The Shakespeare Myth* this political complexion of post-1970 'cultural studies' was made very overt. The book appeared under the general editorship of Alan Sinfield and Jonathan Dollimore, in a series called *Cultural Politics* which explicitly espoused 'cultural materialism' (a development of marxist philosophy) and insisted on its political commitment:

> Cultural materialism does not pretend to political neutrality. It does not, like much established literary criticism, attempt to mystify its perspectives as the natural or obvious interpretation of an allegedly given textual fact. On the contrary, it registers its commitment to the transformation of a social order that exploits people on grounds of race, gender, sexuality and class.

Accordingly *The Shakespeare Myth* was widely received as a political statement, and its impact often described in metaphors of military violence, as in this review[vi]:

> Graham Holderness's collection of essays, bent on exposing the ideological context of 'bardolatry' – both inside and outside of academe – is a well-directed, well-meant volley in the Political Shakespeare[vii] war declared by Terence Hawkes, Terry Eagleton, *et alii.*

And another reviewer in *Shakespeare Survey* described the book as manifesting[viii]

> The embattled and sometimes embittered air of a document from the front line in a war against Thatcher's Britain.

The Shakespeare Myth was indeed polemical, though not quite as parochial as this hostile reviewer implied. Certainly much of my work in the field of 'cultural materialism' derived from studies in marxist philosophy and politics, and owed something to the nature of political engagement as it was then practised on the British left (something of this history is traced here in Chapter 2). But work of the kind represented here was also responsive to more general changes in the scope and competence of literary criticism. One particularly strong emphasis in advanced literary studies, throughout the 1970s and beyond, was on the possibilities of interdisciplinary research, generated by an active dialogue between academic disciplines. Thus specialists in literature and historical studies, linguistics and philosophy, cultural and media studies were in the 1970s coming together, in conferences and journals, in a way that had not happened before, but has become much more familiar since. In particular, Cultural Studies, as an independent discipline, has come of age, being now well established in many universities. The discipline often remains politicised but in a far more general way than the socialist commitment of earlier practitioners: more likely to be concerned with issues of gender, sexual and racial politics than with questions of economy, party or government.[ix]

The essays that follow are characterised as much by this interdisciplinary tendency, and by the opening up of literary studies to a broader cultural critique, as they are by the occasional stridency of their attempts at political engagement. It was the intellectual liberation provided by Cultural Studies (together with the expanding disciplinary boundaries of literature, history, theatre studies, media studies, sociology) that enabled these essays to address such a wide range of 'Shakespearean' topics, from bardolatry to beer-mats, from Westminster Abbey to the 'Bardcard', from the RSC to supermarket sherry. And it was the new plurality of methodologies facilitated by a convergence of disciplines that prompted 'Eng. Lit.' specialists to extend their textual analysis to encompass cultural discourses and social practices; and to eagerly adopt new methods of analysing these phenomena, such as semiotics and the critique of ideology. Hence the essays in this volume are able productively to address such 'extra-textual' topics as the 1951 Festival of Britain and the 'Bardfest' of 1994; the tourist map of Stratford and the struggle over the sites of the Globe and Rose theatres; the image of Shakespeare as it appears on banknotes and credit cards, beer mats and sherry bottles. Some of the later essays, especially Chapters Four, Five and Six, begin to develop the analysis in relation to profoundly significant debates on the nature of nationality, using the Shakespeare 'myth' as a framework for analysis of British national culture.

I have edited the essays lightly, removing irrelevant cross-references, making corrections, omitting passages I now believe to be wrong or misguided, but not attempting to dislocate them from the context of their formation. The final piece, 'Everybody's Shakespeare', published here for the first time, began life as a Professorial lecture. I have not tampered with its expository style, in the hope that it may prove a useful and accessible introduction to the field.

PART ONE

Theory

CHAPTER ONE

Production (1988)

Thee, SHAKESPEARE, today we honour

Since England bore thee, the master of human song ...
One with thee is our temper in melancholy or might
And in thy book Great Britain's rule readeth her right.

Robert Bridges (1916)

THE JINGOISM OF this former Poet Laureate's tribute to Shakespeare, written when England was at war with Germany and clearly designed to validate, by reference to Shakespeare, England's role in that murderous conflict, serves as a useful starting point for an address to the position of Shakespeare within British culture. For centuries the centrality and value within 'English' culture of the canonised works of Shakespeare stood unquestioned. Today new kinds of critical inquiry, new modes of address to the cultural activities of literature and drama, have begun to challenge that time-honoured pre-eminence. True, there have always been isolated acts of irreverent iconoclasm: parodies, spoofs, lampoons and satires, or more concerted critical counterblasts like that of Tolstoi. These spasmodic yelpings of the cultural underdog could always be easily assimilated, since they attempted to operate within the same framework of assumptions as the established hegemonic apparatus of bar-

dolatry: sick of hearing how 'great' Shakespeare was, a few voices
plaintively cried in the wilderness, hoping to de-consecrate the
Bard's divinity and expose his feet of clay. We can no longer simply and innocently applaud and reverence Shakespeare the man,
the dramatist, the national Bard, as the Victorian and Edwardian
imperialists could. Neither can we undertake a straightforward
strategy of revaluation, with the aim of toppling Shakespeare
from his lofty pedestal, or of establishing for other writers alternative claims to cultural authority. We are today much more conscious of the existence of a separable cultural phenomenon:
'Shakespeare' the cultural construction, the ideological force, the
myth. Indeed, the capitalisation of SHAKESPEARE in Robert
Bridges' Tercentenary Ode, quoted above, may indicate that the
possibility of separating man from myth had occurred even to
some of his most sycophantic worshippers. It has now become
possible, with the advance of progressive critical methodologies,
to complete that process of splitting the SHAKESPEARE myth
from Shakespeare the man: to detach from the writing and the
reputation a history of cultural reconstruction, in the active
process of which we can observe 'Shakespeare' being appropriated in the service of various ideologies and political interests. Our
critical attention can thus be transferred from the literary or dramatic texts and their historical conditions of production, to the
cultural apparatus in which they have been ideologically
mobilised: we can now study not just Shakespeare but also
SHAKESPEARE and 'Shakespeare': not just the Shakespeare
canon or the Shakespearean stage but the Shakespeare industry,
the Shakespeare institution, the Shakespeare myth. As Terry
Eagleton has observed,

> Shakespeare is today less an author than an apparatus – his name
> is merely metonymic of an entire politico-cultural formation, and
> thus more akin to 'Disney' or 'Rockefeller' than to 'Jane Smith' ...
> The apparatus has long achieved autonomy of whatever individ-
> ual gave rise to it in the first place; if the shrines of Knock and
> Lourdes could be brought into existence by a non-person, a con-

struct of such institutions rather than an authorial source, then the Shakespeare industry may equally connive to constitute and reconstitute its own 'founder' in an inviolably self-referential gesture.[1]

Shakespeare, it has always been claimed, can make us wise, and good, and free. On the contrary, 'Shakespeare' can, radical criticism is beginning to suggest, operate to delude, to corrupt and to enslave.

◦

On the basis of developments in marxist, post-structuralist, semiotic, feminist, psychoanalytic and cultural-materialist criticism, this operation of demystifying Shakespeare is already well under way in Britain, in the work of an impressive array of critics such as Terry Hawkes, Terry Eagleton, Alan Sinfield, John Drakakis and parallel efforts are being undertaken elsewhere, especially in the United States.[2] The present essay aspires to be a contribution to that process and a pointer towards areas of enquiry where much further work needs to be attempted. One particular field where these advances in critical methodology need to be extended and pressed home, is the investigation of Shakespeare in 'production': a broad context of inquiry which encompasses film and television, textual and theatrical production, and extends further into the social organisation and political valency of culture.

In British cultural conditions this project has encountered a number of methodological difficulties, rooted in turn in certain historical divisions of labour that have accompanied the development of British academic culture. The new critical approaches, from structuralism onwards, which began to penetrate British academic discourse from the early 1970s, tended to find a 'natural' home within institutions and departments of 'Literature', while simultaneously influencing fields of inquiry which had already to one degree or another broken away from the would-be hegemonic apparatus of literary studies – linguistics, cultural studies, film, media and communications studies. Prior to the post-structuralist 'revolution', British literary studies had been dominated jointly by Cambridge English (*Scrutiny* and F.R. Leavis) and by American New Criticism, both schools obsessed with evaluation and with textuality: with the process of privileging the morally beneficial and aesthetically 'great', and with textualised language as the concrete embodiment of experiential meaning. Neither method had anything useful to say about drama: the fact that a great deal of what is conventionally designated 'literature' (including the work of the 'greatest' English author) is actually performance art, was conveniently ignored or the 'dramatic' was theoretically collapsed into the subject-centred process of textual reading.

It was partly as a consequence of this combination of indifference and hostility on the part of literary-critical establishments and institutions that 'Drama' began to emerge as an independent discipline: in the form of autonomous sections within English departments or as separate departments with their own distinct philosophy and method. 'Drama' as an academic subject – now quite widely taught in public sector higher education – drew for its formation on a number of different sources: on the literary criticism from which it sought to detach itself; on historical studies, in the form of an architectural and archaeological concern with 'theatre history'; on Education, which had fostered, on the basis of experiments in early schooling, a powerful philosophy of Drama as a morally and spiritually developmental force; and on the more 'practical' or professionally oriented 'performance arts' – Drama, Music and Dance for acting, voice and movement skills, Art for costume and stage design.

Since the primary target of post-structuralist criticism has been the text-centred approaches of *Scrutiny* and New Criticism, Drama could be seen as an already partially liberated area. There is nothing new or surprising in many of the propositions of post-structuralist theory for Drama specialists, who become understandably irritated at the laborious expositions of post-struc-turalist critics striving to demonstrate that the work of Ben Jon-son is iterable and pluralistic. Drama teachers have in a sense always known, from the very nature of their subject, though they may have used a very different language to formulate their knowledge, that 'reading' is an active process of constructing meaning, not a passive assimilation of encoded truths; that his-torical institutions and practices are important not as a shadowy 'background' to the corporeality of texts but as constitutive deter-minants of those texts and their reproduction; that the meanings of dramatic texts are never stable and authoritative but always (and perhaps infinitely) deconstructable. At the same time, an awareness that the 'language' of drama involves a much wider range of signifying practices has made Drama a natural home for developments in semiotics.

These observations should not, however, lead us to conclude that drama is, or is generally organised and communicated as, a 'naturally' radical art or cultural study: although some of its most eminent practitioners have argued as much. The very eclecticism of the discipline renders it capable of both radical intervention and conservative reproduction: its scholarship and 'theatre histo-ry' can be dominated by nostalgia and escapism; its 'practical' ele-ment can often be reduced either to therapeutic play or to mere training for professional success; its interpretative strategies can be as formalistic as those of literary criticism, and its educational theories are frequently escape hatches to all manner of weird and wonderful notions about self and human nature. In current pro-posals emanating from the Conservative Thatcher government to establish a 'national curriculum' for schools, Drama – along with other 'performance arts' – is marginalised almost into non-exis-tence. The ideologues of Drama claim that this proposed act of suppression by educational policy indicates the truly radical char-acter of Drama as an activity. David Hornbrook has argued on the contrary that this marginalisation is not, as we would like to

think, because Drama is perceived as a potent and dangerous rev-
olutionary force, but because, from an already weak power-base,
it has come to be associated with the kind of woolly thinking and
vague, semi-mystical psychologising that a new Conservative
'purposefulness' intends to eliminate from the curriculum.[3]

Contemporary work on Shakespeare in performance is dominated by methods derived from traditional literary studies: the
hegemonic discourse of this particular cultural practice derives
from a *rapprochement* of activities such as textual scholarship,
interpretative criticism, subject-centred 'reading' and journalistic
reviewing. 'Literature' specialists dominate the columns of the
academic reviews and the various publication projects which
address the analysis of Shakespeare in performance. That fact in
itself does not, of course, invalidate or even compromise the
quality of individual contributions but, in terms of large-scale
cultural analysis, it is clear that the initiative in this area has been
taken by literature so that even the radical potentialities of Drama
have not been incorporated into this area of work.

I am proposing that Drama should recapture this initiative
from English. The investigation of Shakespeare in performance
should be supported by a serious engagement with post-structuralist criticism for the interpretation of dramatic literature;
with cultural sociology, for analysis of the institutional and ideological contexts of theatre production; with history, both for a
broader cultural perspective and for an understanding of the
nature of theatrical spaces, audiences, ideologies; with theatre
semiotics, for methods of decoding the signifying practices of
drama; with practical experimentation, for concrete explorations
of the pluralistic character of all performance art; with politics,
both in a general sense and in relation to specific issues of race,
sexuality and gender; and with progressive currents in film and
media studies, where examples of theoretical rigour can take the
analysis of drama on the screen far beyond the flabby platitudes
of current criticism and reviewing. Only through the appropria-

tion of these and other methodologies will Drama be able to re-establish itself as a discipline with something important and con-vincing to say, rather than as an ancillary craft, a fringe philosophy or a Victorian 'lady's accomplishment'.

∞

At the centre of any consideration of Shakespeare in performance must lie the curious phenomenon of the Royal Shakespeare Company, that huge national institution which receives millions of pounds in state subsidy to produce the dramatic works of Shakespeare. The RSC could not have been created in the shape that it was, a permanent company formulated around the work of one particular dramatist, if that dramatist had not already grown into a national institution in his own right. However, there can be little doubt that the RSC now functions as one of the principal agencies for maintaining the unique privileged role for Shake-speare as the British national Bard. The RSC actually shares the position of 'state theatre' with the formally titled National on the South Bank: both jointly occupy a uniquely prestigious and privi-leged space within the apparatus of centralised metropolitan cul-ture; both, together with the Royal Opera House, receive unparalleled generosity from the state's machinery of arts fund-ing; both function as centres of excellence promulgating the highest levels of cultural production both home and abroad, to native and foreign visitors; and both are deeply imbricated within the ideological structures of the British national state. Indeed, in the earliest stages of their conception the convergence of ideolog-ical interests between the two institutions might have led to their becoming one.

In the mid-nineteenth century the first proposer of the plan for a national theatre, a London publisher called Effingham Wilson, called his project 'a House for Shakespeare'. Wilson, a free-thinking radical dissenter, conceived his model of national

theatre as an antidote and an alternative to the commercial theatre of the West End: it should exist to place serious plays, the
great classical heritage of British drama, within the reach of ordinary working people and should not be confined to London but
should have theatres in all the major cities throughout Britain.
'Shakespeare' in this scenario actually symbolised those cultural
treasures long since appropriated by the aristocracy, but capable
of re-appropriation on behalf of a petit-bourgeois popular culture. The nineteenth century origins of the RSC were curiously
parallel: the Shakespeare Memorial Theatre in Stratford-upon-
Avon was built and endowed by Flowers, the wealthy local brewing family, who like Effingham Wilson had a history of religious
dissent and liberal politics. Before 1960 the theatre became merely
a seasonal venue for London-based companies but the Flowers'
original aspiration was that it should house a subsidised permanent ensemble company modelled on that of the Duke of Saxe-
Meiningen. At a time when the business of drama was wholly
commercial and when acting companies were hierarchical structures dominated by the great actor-managers, the voices of these
far-sighted liberal-bourgeois visionaries were demanding a
national theatre to be fostered and funded by the state; organised
around the concept of a permanent subsidised ensemble; centred
on the work of Shakespeare and playing to the whole 'nation'
rather than to a tiny minority of the cultivated élite in London. In
retrospect we can recognise these ambitions and ideals within the
historical framework of a large-scale bourgeois-democratic cultural revolution which, from the 1840s onwards, began to consolidate the political gains of the ascendant class and to challenge the
old regime to a battle over the cultural meanings of the past.

The campaign for a National Theatre had a long and tortuous
history but in 1960 Peter Hall seized the initiative on behalf of
Stratford and succeeded in securing state funding for a permanent Royal Shakespeare Company, based in Stratford but with a
lease on a London theatre; founded on Shakespeare but with a

commitment to commissioning and performing new theatrical writing; an artistic centre of excellence with a strong sense of social responsibility and political consciousness. The precise nature and degree of the RSC's early 'radicalism' has been seriously questioned by some penetrating cultural-materialist studies which have suggested that it was never more than superficial and cosmetic.[4] The fact remains that in 1960 a new kind of theatrical organisation came into being: which departed from the prevailing 'star' system and founded itself on the ensemble principles learned from the Moscow Art Theatre and the Berliner Ensemble; which was liberated by state subsidy from commercial pressures, and therefore free to experiment and innovate; which accepted a commitment to keep classical and new writing in some kind of creative inter-relationship; and which was sufficiently responsive to political issues to earn sustained and systematic criticism from many who regarded the company as subversive of political orthodoxy and artistic tradition. Though very much a product of its time, the early RSC incorporated some of the more radical suggestions of the bourgeois-democratic proponents of a national theatre so that, despite its unquestionable position at the centre of national culture, the RSC could justifiably claim to represent, albeit in a remote and distanced way, rather more of the actual 'nation' than could ever be represented by a purely classical repertory company.

Many of the RSC's activities over almost thirty years of its existence have been in keeping with this cultural continuity, this effort to sustain the radical values of an earlier ideological battle. The company has diversified its operations into very different spaces such as the Other Place and the Swan in Stratford, or the Pit at the Barbican Centre. These smaller 'studio' or 'private theatre' spaces have fostered some of the most interesting and creative work the company has achieved. A policy of touring has taken the RSC out of the confined cultural milieu of the capital and within reach of the experience of a larger national constituency, even establishing alternative home bases such as the north-east.[5] The company's theatre-in-education work has diversified activities and expanded the range of possible ways of perceiving the cultural heritage, the legacy of the past.

It is often difficult, in the case of an institution with such a complex and contradictory history, to define precisely what directions of development and change seem to represent the future configuration of its cultural structure and effectiveness. However, as the RSC moves into the 1990s, the writing seems to be inscribed very clearly on the wall. The RSC has expanded to such an extent and, has become such a large and complex corporation, that even a current increase in state funding is not sufficient to cover its operating costs. Two methods of resolving this financial shortfall have been adopted by the company: the production of hit musicals which can make the lucrative transfer to Broadway and a search for corporate sponsorship. In 1987 this resulted in a large insurance company, Royal Insurance, paying off the RSC's £1,000,000 deficit. Such acts of corporate generosity do not come without strings: the RSC is now 'sponsored by Royal Insurance'; committed to making, at the sponsor's behest, a 'Royal Insurance' tour; and its theatrical activities will, of course, begin to be shaped and influenced by the demands of this or any other private sponsor. The original virtue of state subsidy was that it left a company relatively free from commercial pressures. The expansion and commercialising of the RSC has led to an increasing dependence on private funding, and hence perhaps to the beginning of a process by which the arts are returned directly into the control of British big business and international capital. The original idea of a national theatre was that it should offer a genuine alternative to the crude commercialism of the West End. Now the RSC has joined the West End theatres in the competition to launch the most profitable hit musical.

꙳

In Britain 'Shakespeare on Television' is almost synonymous with the BBC/Time-Life Shakespeare series which, between 1979 and 1986, broadcast the entire series of thirty-seven plays. This huge Anglo-American project, by means of which the centralised British institution of communications was able to tap into both the resources of its own national culture and the capacious purses of American private enterprise, has succeeded in establishing itself as the pre-eminently 'English' model for integrating television with Shakespeare, and probably for the foreseeable future blocked any further experimentation, certainly on the part of the BBC, in the adaptation of Shakespeare to the small screen. The series has consistently been publicised and promoted as unique in its scope and scale, and in the massive investment of cultural and commercial capital it necessarily entailed. Paradoxically its huge commercial publicity and marketing operation, and its remorselessly monumental classicising of both the plays and the concept of British culture into which they were assimilated, have come to seem like the only 'natural' way to put Shakespeare on television, and have obscured much more important and interesting diversities and variations within the medium of television and within the range of techniques and conventions available for television dramatisation.[6]

Television 'drama' is, of course, a much broader and more heterogeneous field of production than the familiar long-established category of 'drama' as it exists in the theatre. However, the BBC/Time-Life Shakespeare series operated from the outset on the basis of a determination to isolate the productions and the series from the conventions and the medium of television drama. As Raymond Williams argued,[7] the nature of the television medium in all developed societies involves a movement away from the transmission of discrete and independent programme units, such as 'plays', and towards a coherent and connected 'flow' of programmed material. The actual 'broadcasting' comes to consist less in the nature of the independent units and more in the character of that integrated and programmed flow. The natural rhythm of 'drama' on television is in fact serial, an extended and sustained development in which each unit establishes its own 'interestingness' partly by drawing on previous episodes and partly by stimulating interest in what is to follow. The fact that many examples of this technique (such as the big American soap operas) are tedious and trivial, is no reflection on the serial mode itself. Anyone who considers the serial mode to be 'inartistic' has not considered the historical examples of Greek tragedy and medieval European religious drama or the nineteenth century novel; and has not reflected on the calibre of some of the dramatic writers who have devised serial plays for television – Howard Brenton, Dennis Potter, Trevor Griffiths.

The 'unity' of the BBC Shakespeare series was not this pluralistic and overdetermined unity of the television medium but the cultural homogeneity of the British Broadcasting Corporation itself. The programmers did everything possible to isolate each individual production from the natural programmed 'flow' of the television medium, to protect these monumental emblems of our classical heritage from contamination by the trivial and transitory detritus of our quotidian popular culture. The plays were broadcast at a special symbolic time, the Sunday evening 'slot' traditionally reserved by the BBC for material of a religious or morally edifying nature. Each production was heralded and pre-publicised by write-ups in the *Radio Times*, the BBC's programming magazine, dealing variously with the play, the director, the actors and the production. Each production was further promoted and defensively flanked, both on BBC radio and television, by half-hour introductory talks and programmes involving actors, writers, broadcasters, journalists and academics discussing aspects of the play or detailing their own relationship with Shakespeare. These were subsequently published in a two-volume companion book, *Shakespeare in Perspective*.[8] In addition, a special text of the complete plays (actually nothing more than the familiar Alexander text augmented by the addition of introductions by the Literary Consultant to the series, John Wilders, and by notes on the production itself) was published by the BBC as a supplement or companion to the series, thus completing the constituent materials of a highly marketable 'package'.

Apologists for the series argue that this strategy of encircling a production with explanatory, interpretative and anecdotal publicity was a necessary device of mediation, designed to assist the 'uneducated' viewer in the task of understanding and appreciating unfamiliar and dauntingly difficult plays. It is also pointed out that the series was from the outset conceived as an educational enterprise, both directly in the sense that the marketable 'package' of video cassettes and ancillary publications was aimed ultimately at institutions of education, and indirectly in its historical connection with the BBC's traditional role as custodian of the nation's moral and educational standards. Lastly, since the series owes its origins to American cultural and commercial co-operation, a concern was optimistically maintained for the intelligibility threshold of the average Mexican peon.

Whatever the motives for the employment of these cultural strategies, their effect was to distinguish the Shakespeare series very sharply, in terms of character and of quality, from anything else the BBC or other television networks might produce. It attempted a popularisation and publicising of the series by making the viewing of each broadcast production into a special occasion or significant event more akin to a theatre visit than to a televisual experience. The curiously old-fashioned air of the series, which sits oddly besides its aggressive and entrepreneurial marketing approach, has much to do with this dependence on the cultural ambience and conventions of another medium, the theatre. It is many years since broadcasting institutions ceased to think of their medium in terms of its original uses, as primarily a method of *transmitting* a live event to places remote from its enactment. But the BBC Shakespeare series, by planning the broadcasts for significant moments, attempting to excite through ancillary broadcasts and publicity the viewer's expectations of a rich and rewarding cultural experience, and providing various kinds of souvenir 'programme' material, sought to emulate the social and cultural rituals of theatre-going: not, it should be emphasised, by mixing the conventions of each medium or by provoking a dialectical interaction between them but merely by seeking to draw the spectator into a social ritual akin to the devotee's reverential pilgrimage to a theatre.

Contrary to current received wisdom, there are many other ways of adapting Shakespeare to the medium of television; alternative strategies of cultural reproduction which need not necessarily entail such a wholesale surrender to the values of high culture and commercial success as the BBC/Time-Life series represents. In fact, BBC TV itself in its early days attempted rather different methods of putting Shakespeare on the small screen. The earliest experiments in televising Shakespeare in the 1930s took the form of broadcasting selected 'Scenes from Shakespeare': brief samples of dramatic material more in keeping with the other dramatic, non-fictional and light entertainment programmes the medium was offering. Not only was there no attempt to dramatise the whole canon, the programmes did not even record complete plays. The British independent television networks have rarely attempted Shakespeare productions but as it happens, the production widely regarded as one of the best screen adaptations of a Shakespeare play ever made, the 1979 version of Trevor Nunn's *Macbeth*, originated as the filming, by an independent video company, of a stage production which then appeared on Thames Television in the form of a serial of half-a-dozen episodes broadcast for schools. The new Channel Four offered its own alternative to the BBC Shakespeare series by commissioning director Michael Bogdanov to televise a series of theatre workshops in which National Theatre actors and an invited audience rehearsed, improvised, adapted and discussed six

Shakespeare plays. All these examples have one thing in common: they sought and found ways of adapting Shakespeare to the medium of television, rather than forcing the medium to come to terms with 'Shakespeare'.

೩ಿ

A rather different kind of theatrical intervention, no less instructive and enlightening as to the priorities and the fate of British 'liberal' culture in the late 1980s, is the International Shakespeare Globe Trust, a charitable organisation dedicated to rebuilding the Globe Theatre on London's Bankside. Modelled, both in its conception and its techniques of fundraising and administration, on similar American ventures, the London Globe reconstruction project can, of course, claim a unique and unchallengeable advantage: its replica of 'Shakespeare's theatre' will stand on or near the original theatre's conjectural site beside the Thames and close to the modern Southwark Bridge. Masterminded by the American actor and director Sam Wanamaker, the 'Southwark Globe' project has earned considerable academic and scholarly respect, as well as a great deal of publicity and substantial sums of money. However, both the basic concept of the reconstruction and its turbulent history through the two decades of its existence need to be re-addressed in the light of our present interest in the 'Shakespeare' industry.[9]

Several different motives, all of which are combined in Sam Wanamaker's eclectic and enthusiastic interest in the living history of the theatre, underlie the formation of the project, and indirectly influence both the shape of its organisation and the likely configuration of its eventual cultural policy. There is a scholarly and academic ambition to re-establish as accurately as possible the physical conditions which produced Elizabethan drama. Leading theatre historians were recruited into the project's network of advisory committees and engaged to produce detailed reports on the architecture of the original Globe theatre in order to secure the most reliable and authoritative advice on its reconstruction. There is a theatrical practitioner's interest in a replica Renaissance theatre usable for dramatic experimentation. There is an educationalist's wish to provide a demonstrative model of a Renaissance institution for pedagogic purposes. There is an antiquarian concern to develop a museum of the Elizabethan/ Jacobean stage. Lastly, there is the proposition to inaugurate a new tourist centre, in competition with London's other 'heritage' attractions and with Stratford-upon-Avon, to act (in the words of the project's newsletter *The Southwark Globe*) 'as a Mecca for the millions of Shakespeare lovers from all over the world'. Clearly all these aspirations could be satisfied by building a replica Renaissance theatre anywhere in the world, save the last: for it is only as a reconstruction occupying the theatre's original site that the Globe project could enter into competition with other historic monuments and bid for a space on the highly competitive tourist itinerary of modern London. Although the underlying motivations are varied and complex, it could be argued that its commercial centre consists of an entrepreneurial thrust into the tourist industry. It is this aspect that accounts for the difficult history of the project, and that must ultimately cast serious political doubt over its chances of fulfilling its other objectives.

Since the Globe project depends for its funding (estimated at some £15,000,000) on private patronage and commercial sponsorship, it exists at one level as a large-scale public relations exercise, through which Wanamaker courted the capitalists of America and Japan, appropriating profit and converting it to culture. At the other end of the project's lines of communication lay a different public relations problem. The piece of derelict riverside property intended to house the Globe, although previously purchased by the Globe Trust, lay within, and was subject to, local government laws and regulations: it formed the site for a municipal roadsweepers' depot. The Globe could not be built without the permission of the local government authority, the Council of the London Borough of Southwark. From the outset Wanamaker established links with the Southwark Council, a Labour-controlled authority, and promoted the Globe reconstruction as a community project, an initiative in urban renewal which would develop the area and benefit the inhabitants of what is the third poorest local authority in England.

> We were seeking the kind of community participation that would keep us informed of and sensitive to local needs ... We had a local community committee, we always saw ourselves as having two faces: one looking north, across the river to the wider world beyond; the other facing south to the locality, and to the people of Southwark and the other London boroughs. We never abandoned the belief that we were local, national and international in character.[10]

Initially, the bona fides of this 'community' project was accepted by the ruling Labour group in Southwark Council, who entered a tri-partite agreement between the Trust and a property developer interested in the commercial potentialities of the site, and granted planning permission for the building of the Globe. Shortly afterwards, however, local elections brought a more decisively left-wing Labour group into power in Southwark and the tide of opinion promptly turned against the Globe. To the new council the project had no discernible community benefit at all but represented an alliance of commercial exploiters and cultural entrepreneurs, determined to establish on the site an élitist centre of high culture and a profitable tourist interest. The council argued that the site should be used directly for the people and the community: it should continue to house the roadsweepers and should at some time in the future be used for public housing. On the basis of a legal technicality the council reneged on their agreement with the Globe Trust and thereby precipitated a legal conflict.

The Globe Trust emerged victorious from that lawsuit with permission to build the Globe and the council (ultimately the citizens of Southwark) inherited the unenviable task of paying the property developer £7.7 million pounds in compensation for breach of contract. Whether or not the Globe project could ever have developed into a genuinely local, popular, community enterprise, remains an open question. What is certain is that in the course of this battle with the local council the more democratic and egalitarian aspirations of the Globe Trust became noticeably attenuated, and the more élitist and commercial motivations came to the fore. The roadsweepers' depot – headquarters of a highly necessary social service, staffed by perfectly respectable and bona fide members of Southwark's 'local community' – became in the publicity of the Globe Trust's defensive campaign, a powerful symbol: a ludicrous example of high art and respectable culture being encumbered and obstructed by the contemptible detritus, human and material, of a modern industrial society. The Globe's public relations personnel evidently perceived no contradiction between their populist rhetoric, their vision of the Shakespearean theatre as transcendent of social divisions and class barriers, and their instinctive antipathy to the concrete representatives of that very democratic culture the project claims to serve. Roadsweepers must, apparently, like the chimney sweepers in Shakespeare's beautifully democratic lyric, 'come to dust' while the immortal spirit of Shakespeare, reincarnated in the brick and timber of a mock-Tudor replica theatre, endures for ever.

The Spring 1987 issue of the *Southwark Globe* carried on its front a picture of the Duke of Edinburgh presenting a 'royal oak' from Windsor Great Park to form one of the theatre's foundation posts. The Conservative government's Arts Minister, Richard Luce, offered a description of the project interestingly different from Sam Wanamaker's populist vision of a community arts project:

It is indeed, the most enterprising of ventures. The original Globe theatre was one of the earliest joint-stock companies, and this project will follow with the same enterprising spirit.

In the dialect of monetarist culture, Shakespeare's theatre appears as a model of capitalist enterprise. John Lee, Conservative Minister for tourism, was also there to locate the Globe onto the London tourist circuit. The same issue of the trust's newsletter carried a report on a conference held in February 1987 on 'Southwark tourism', in which tourism was proposed as a remedy for unemployment and in which 'all speakers welcomed the Globe as a wonderful asset to North Southwark'. Thus the Globe project has clearly shifted its public position from attachment to an unsympathetic local authority to dependence on the local business community, the Royal family and the Tory government. Its aspirations to represent the revival of popular theatre and the rehabilitation of an economically derelict area have become subordinated to the commercial and touristic components of the enterprise.

All these artistic developments clearly take their form from the general cultural conditions of Thatcherite Britain in the late 1980s, which derive in turn from economic and political priorities of a reactionary monetarist policy. For the first time since the end of the Second World War, a government has set itself the task of dismantling the entire British cultural apparatus and reconstructing it in the light of Thatcherite wisdom. Parallel with the privatisation of state industries, the long struggle to abolish effective trades unions and the gradual dismantling of the welfare state, Tory approaches to education and the arts have sought to replace independence and state funding with ministerial control and privatisation. In this general context of cultural politics, the specific modes of development identified in the RSC, the BBC and the Globe trust seem easily anticipated signs of the times. In such conditions of cultural struggle, where the historical past as well as the political present, is a site of contestation for meaning between competing appropriations, it is vital that we be aware of the ever-present potentialities for cultural progress and democratic change. If there is a struggle for meaning over the body of 'Shakespeare', we cannot simply surrender the past to the forces of reaction. To develop the kind of dialectical methodology I have advocated – which can simultaneously challenge and subvert reactionary appropriations of 'Shakespeare', and disclose and foster those enterprises of recovery that can use Shakespeare for the purpose of advancing critical social awareness and vigilant political consciousness – seems to me an urgent priority of progressive cultural politics.

CHAPTER TWO

Reproduction (1991)

৵

PROGRESSIVE CULTURAL WORK has frequently been marked by exhortations to theorise and historicise the activity of the 'critic' (an ideologically loaded term which might more appropriately be replaced by other figurative personae – the writer, the reader, the teacher): to reflect self-consciously on the practices of politically radical cultural analysis. This motivation towards self-exposure which derives from a theoretical rejection of the pseudo-objectivity characteristic of traditional forms of criticism, from a methodological acknowledgement that a criticism committed to disclosing the ideological infrastructure of cultural works cannot operate by concealing its own ideological problematic, and from a 'post-modernist' preoccupation with meta-discourse has featured strongly in specifically focused feminist writing, but in other areas has remained relatively undeveloped. Walter Cohen's pioneering essay 'Political criticism of Shakespeare' (1987[1]) is therefore an important contribution to a necessary operation: the observations I wish to make about it should be received in the context of an applauding recognition of its decisive significance for politically conscious work in the cultural field.

Cohen's detailed and extensive discussion on the growth and development of 'political criticism' in Renaissance studies provides a model example for the cultural analysis of academic and educational institutions, and shows a critic beginning to take seriously the post-structuralist imperative to investigate and identify all ideological positions, including our own. In the course of his analysis Cohen suggests some points of distinction between 'political criticisms' as they are practised on opposite sides of the Atlantic, in Britain and in North America. Through the contrasting influences of New Criticism, with its cultivation of 'emotional distance' between reader and text and Leavisite criticism, with its insistence on moral commitment, British criticism emerges from such a comparison inflected by 'a far greater orientation towards the present and toward explicitly political concerns than one finds in the United States' (p. 21). 'British Marxist discussions of Shakespeare' are thus characterised by a combination of traditional and innovative practices: 'a revisionist historical analysis of the plays in their own time and a radical account of their ideological function in the present' (p. 27). Surveying the 'far smaller field of American Marxist writing on Shakespeare', Cohen asserts that 'none of these critics even address the issue that British Marxists have successfully begun to explore: the contemporary institutional force and social function of Shakespeare'.

This seems to me a key distinction between forms of critical enterprise which, although cognate, convergent and closely interlinked, are moving increasingly into positions of mutual antagonism and conflict. But what divides them is not entirely or necessarily geographical location. If we are looking for examples of this kind of politically engaged contemporary focus on Renaissance reproductions, it would certainly be to British cultural work that we would look: to Simon Barker's 'Images of the sixteenth and seventeenth centuries as a history of the present', to the second half of *Political Shakespeare*, to *The Shakespeare myth*, to the work of Hawkes and Evans and Drakakis[2]. By contrast the work that is currently dominating the American Renaissance journals, either directly or in the form of recuperative opposition, has its gaze firmly located on the past, if only by virtue of an attention to contemporary intellectual work that is itself a processing of history.

The critical anthology in which Cohen's essay appears seems to mediate between these competing tendencies. An international, though predominantly American product, emanating from the International Shakespeare Congress held in West Berlin in 1986, *Shakespeare reproduced* is co-edited by two women, one American and one British (Jean Howard and Marion O'Connor). It contains eleven contributions from America, two from the former GDR (East Germany) and one from Britain. Most of the contributions adopt what is by now a familiar form, the discussion of one play in relation to the literary and philosophical problems and methods of deconstruction, feminist and psychoanalytic criticism, race, politics, history. While these are in their way impressive pieces of work, they leave a sense of unfulfilment: not simply because they operate within a well-tried professional format, but because the editors and contributors are continually promising or demanding something more[3]:

> Other work beckons, as well. We need examinations of Shakespeare's use at all levels of the educational system, and not just in colleges and universities; and we need to investigate the ideological use of Shakespeare in other wide-reaching cultural practices such as television and film. But even then, we would argue, the work of a political and historical criticism of Shakespeare will not be done. Shakespeare is constantly reproduced in the general discourses of culture and is used to authorise practices as diverse as buying perfume, watching Masterpiece Theatre, or despatching troops to far-flung corners of the globe. We need studies which consider particular uses of the name or image of Shakespeare or of Shakespearean play titles, speeches or snippets of verse in advertising, in popular culture magazines, in political rhetoric. Ignoring these uses of Shakespeare as trivial or beyond our expertise means acquiescing in the separation of the academy from general culture and means ignoring, as well, much of what in our own time may be of significance to a political and historical criticism.

Few of the writers actually address these issues. The one contribution that really takes the volume into new territory is Marion F.
O'Connor's examination of the 'Shakespeare's England' exhibition at Earl's Court in 1912: 'Theatre of the Empire'[4]. This fasci-
nating essay moves quite beyond the well-trodden paths of
textual re-reading to the elaborate decoding of another kind of
text, one of those significant 'reproductions' of Shakespeare with
which the volume as a whole so clearly fails to engage. Moving
from society costume balls, through the productions of William
Poel's Elizabethan Stage Society, Queen Victoria's Jubilee, *Country Life Illustrated* and the architectural style of Edward Lutyens,
O'Connor takes us to view the simulated reconstructions of
Drake's *Revenge* and Shakespeare's Globe Theatre at an exhibition
which expresses vividly and eloquently the spirit of imperial
Britain shortly before the First World War. In place of the 'arbitrary connectedness' which Walter Cohen identifies as the key
method and the structural weakness of 'New Historicism'[5],
O'Connor links her diversified and disparate elements into a
powerful analysis of ideological and institutional reproduction.
This is 'history', of course, but formulated in terms of a cultural
historiography that looks far beyond a distanced, periodised
'Renaissance', to the institutional origins and concrete forms
of cultural reproduction in a particular, relatively accessible,
'present'.

The strategies and methods of such a cultural historiography
can easily be applied to a contemporary process of Renaissance
reproduction in which other Globe theatres, other royal jubilees,
other wars, continue to be implicated; the political repercussions
of such study are correspondingly direct and unmistakable. The
contrast with 'New Historicism', which can describe its motivation as 'a desire to speak with the dead', is extreme. Although
'New Historicism' has frequently in the past been regarded as
indistinguishable from Marxist 'cultural materialism', the true
distance between them is disclosed with particular clarity by the
publication of Stephen Greenblatt's *Shakespearean negotiations*

(1988)[6]. The basic theoretical approach of Greenblatt's 'New Historicism' takes its starting point from an interdisciplinary convergence of literary and historical methodologies. The traditionally constitutive structure of literary understanding – the author, the canon, the organic text – are deconstructed and the dramatic texts returned to the historical culture from which they emanated. The traditionally indispensable techniques of literary investigation – verbal analysis, qualitative identification, evaluation – are largely abandoned in favour of an intertextual juxtapositioning of authorised literary works with the products of 'non-literary' discourses. Other plays and other texts, together with contemporary beliefs and cultural customs, social practices and institutional structures, are continually thrown into an exciting and liberating interplay of discourses, as Greenblatt traces the continuous flow and circulation of ideological forms and political interventions throughout the complex body of Renaissance society. The isolation of Shakespeare as deified author and the strict perimeters of demarcation between Shakespearean texts and other forms of writing, are convincingly broken down, thus opening up Renaissance culture to new methods of literary and historical analysis. The ultimate objective of that analysis is certainly the sphere of the political: through verbal and structural investigation of rhetorical strategies, the critic discloses the conditions of cultural, ideological and political power. The dramatic texts become sites for the negotiation and authorisation, interrogation and subversion, containment and recuperation of the forms of Renaissance power. But the political situation into which those demystified forms are then decanted, the present context of the critical utterance itself, is not specifically an object of address, or is constituted only rhetorically by means of a mannered post-modernist self-consciousness.

Some of the important differences between American 'New Historicism' and British 'cultural materialism' are now through such contrasting examples becoming more clearly visible than they were a mere few years ago. Cultural materialism is much more concerned to engage with contemporary cultural practice, where New Historicism confines its focus of attention to the past. Cultural materialism can be overtly, even stridently, polemical about its political implications, where New Historicism tends to efface them. Cultural materialism partly derives its theory and method from the kind of cultural criticism exemplified by Raymond Williams, and through that inheritance stretches its roots into the British tradition of Marxist cultural analysis, and thence into the wider movement for socialist education and emancipation. New Historicism has no sense of a corresponding political legacy and takes its intellectual bearings directly from 'post-structuralist' theoretical and philosophical models. American 'political' critics seem to think of their ideology as having been formed in the environment of the 1960s campus radicalism – in 'the political crucible of the 1960s'[7]. Their British counterparts are at least as likely to have imbibed their ideological formation from the free milk and orange juice of the post-war socialist reconstruction. Cultural materialism accepts as appropriate objects of enquiry a wide range of 'textual' materials: social rituals, historical objects, material from popular culture, buildings, theatres, actors and actresses, performances of plays. New Historicism concerns itself principally with a narrower definition of the 'textual': with what has been *written* rather than with what has been enacted, performed, uttered, built, organised, collected or exhibited.

Political criticism, like sex, is something you can't do effectively on your own. On this side of the Atlantic the natural form for radical criticism was the critical anthology, the forum for a collaborative but abrasive conjuncture of different voices – the Essex conference on *1642*, *Political Shakespeare*, *Alternative Shakespeares*, *The Shakespeare Myth*.[8] Precisely because Greenblatt's work has been developed within such a system of collaboration, and has appeared so often already in the context of these collective forms, its manifestation in the form of the elegant, urbane and learned monograph seems strikingly to characterise an individual voice, unmistakably distinctive even as it denies its own autonomy.[9]

> I began with the desire to speak with the dead ... It was true that I could hear only my own voice, but my own voice was the voice of the dead, for the dead had contrived to leave textual traces of themselves, and those traces make themselves heard in the voices of the living.

This is not only an individual voice and the voice of an accomplished rhetorician: it is also a highly mannered voice bespeaking a form of cultural authority. Evidently when New Historicism seeks to give utterance to the voices of those witnesses normally eliminated from the history of a culture – the subversive and the oppressed, the marginalised and the dispossessed – it encounters a need simultaneously to adopt a voice capable of contesting power and authority within the apparatus of that very academic institution established to suppress those lost voices.

Walter Cohen effectively accounts for this abstracted quality of New Historicism. In pointing to the moral fervour and non-conformist evangelical zeal of Leavis, he correctly diagnoses one possible route through which a socialist cultural politics found it possible to develop (via that cultural and educational configuration summed up in the useful term 'left-Leavisism'). However, Cohen's analysis fails to account for the most obvious reason for the relatively contemporary focus of attention to be found in British Marxist criticism: a reason which lies in the existence of a British tradition of Marxist literary criticism and Marxist cultural analysis, preceding even the *annus mirabilis* of 1968, certainly pre-dating the incorporation of French theoretical work in the 1970s. Cohen's bibliographical compilation of political studies of Shakespeare[10] takes as its starting point the year 1980. Although he admits that the list is 'arbitrary in its boundaries', that particular *terminus a quo* effectively occludes the historical roots of British Marxist criticism and its specific forms of political engagement. Cohen is aware that in Britain 'leftist cultural criticism developed earlier', but still wishes to nominate 1980 as a 'significant point of demarcation, with an intensified radical response to the recent victory of Thatcher, the extension of this work to Renaissance literature and the publication of an important marxist study of Middleton' (p. 19). That the work of a veteran communist critic and activist such as Margot Heinemann should be regarded as the inception of a new age of theory, rather than as the development and consolidation of a long tradition of Marxist cultural practice, is sufficient indication of the deformation introduced into cultural analysis of the British experience by this particular attempt at periodisation.

I have no wish to isolate this historical continuum, the 'tradition' of British Marxism or to reflect nostalgically on the achievements of that tradition in the 1930s and 1950s, though they are there, and they were mediated into our modern cultural practice by the work and example of Raymond Williams. Still less would I wish to minimise the importance of post-Althusserian Marxist philosophy, its wholesale revision of earlier variants of Marxism, its transformation of terms such as ideology, base and superstructure, humanism, its capacity to enter into dialectical relations with linguistic, psychoanalytic and feminist theories. There are, however, certain other characteristics of that earlier cultural work which might instructively be re-examined. Like Marxist philosophy itself, it took as a model for any kind of political, economic or cultural analysis the unity of theory and practice. Also in keeping with Marxist philosophy, it maintained a constant focus on the political present: there was never any possibility of regarding Marxism, as New Historicism tends to regard it, simply as a means of explaining the past. It was always inseparable from clearly defined political commitment and from direct or indirect political or quasi-political involvement. You would expect a left academic in the late 1960s or early 1970s to be a member of a specific political party – Communist Party, International Socialists (later Socialist Workers' Party), International Marxist Group, Marxist wing of the Labour Party – or at least to be active in those branches of adult and 'political' education which ramified, often through the unions, into the labour movement itself.

I know I will be accused of retrospective political nostalgia. To have been present and politically active in a period, the early 1970s, when the mobilisation of the labour movement could free workers imprisoned for trades union activity, or bring down a Tory government, is to have acquired a concrete awareness of political possibilities that I would not wish to relinquish, even in this dark and bitter time of defeat and retrenchment. I know we cannot revive old policies, or follow an antique drum. But it was certainly in those conditions of direct struggle that I acquired my sense of the inescapably political nature of all culture. Political conditions today are so different as to throw those direct struggles of the early 1970s into sharp historical relief, as the victory of 1974 was eclipsed by the terrible defeat of 1984: where now are the crystal-clear imperatives of political struggle?

Linked to this general crisis and failure of the political will are the philosophical anxieties associated with 'post-modernism'. Setting aside the question of whether a *cultural* theory like postmodernism could really ever be held to compromise and undermine a *political* philosophy like Marxism, it seems to me that the revisionist Marxism we are likely to be holding on to today is not so very different from the Marxism we inherited at the end of the 1960s. It was never, in my experience of Marxist political practice in that period, an item of belief that the proletarian revolution was inevitable. The 'scientific' element in 'scientific socialism' was always subjected to deeply critical question and I can recall very few instances of Marxist analysis or political action that were entirely free from scepticism, relativism and the awareness of manifold possibilities. Certainly we used to construct a 'grand narrative' in which 'history' was imputed to be always and ultimately 'on the side of the people' but 'history' was understood with absolute clarity to be 'nothing more or less than the activity of man pursuing his aims'. Although the subject of that operation would now (correctly) require instantaneous redefinition, the concrete presence in the labour movement of the

early 1970s of militant and articulate women made it abundantly
clear that Marx's generic term for humanity was not in practical
application to be understood as in any way patriarchally inflected. In the Marxist texts themselves (which I used to teach to
workers in Communist Party education classes and in classes for
trades unionists or organised by the Workers' Educational Association), the 'master narrative' describing successive phases of economic development, and adumbrating the final overthrow of
capitalism by socialism, was never read as metaphysical prophecy
but rather as political exhortation. The Marxist philosophy of
history, and the Marxist methods of economic and political
analysis, were means of understanding the developments of the
past. These could then be applied to specific tasks of political
action which would, if successful, realise the political development of the future.

The Marxism that I first absorbed in that critical period was a
Stalinist deformation already de-stabilised by the assault of
Althusserian philosophy, and its interaction with a Hegelian
humanist variation of Marxism developed in resistance to
Althusser. Marxism was very much, in the late 1960s and early
1970s, a philosophy in crisis and change. Politically it contained
and retained a version of the 'Popular Front' strategy of a broad-
based alliance of anti-capitalist groups (one example is the
Communist Party programme known as 'The British Road to
Socialism'). Althusserian Marxism, with its emphasis on the relative autonomy of separable cultural, political and economic
spheres of activity seemed to me to endorse this political strategy
(though it was then, and has subsequently been, interpreted quite
differently, as the vindication of a theoretically empowered van-
guard élite). The key problem was, and still is, whether Marxist
philosophy could ever hope to offer a macro-narrative complex
enough to incorporate this pluralism, without either excluding
or oppressing particular groups which would wish to be part
of the progressive movement, but not on terms which would
marginalise their own interests or becoming so attenuated as to

disappear altogether as a totalising force. My own view is that this project is still perfectly feasible: but then I have always regarded the *analytical* content of Marxist politics – specific analysis of concrete historical situations and applied political strategies designed to realise ultimate objectives – to be far more important than the *theoretical* content of Marxist philosophy. I agree with Jean Howard that very broad 'Enlightenment' categories such as 'universal emancipation' can be used as ultimate goals because the crucial imperative in any historical situation is to co-ordinate, in some broad-based programme, forces capable of working towards both particular and general forms of human emancipation.

What we can carry forward from that earlier tradition of *praxis*, contemporary engagement and direct commitment, into a greatly strengthened and theoretically developed historical materialism, are certain methods of political analysis and cultural intervention. We can draw on the 'empiricist' leanings of an earlier form of Marxism, to re-introduce methods of concrete historical and cultural analysis. Our earlier fears of empiricism seem naive in the context of the New Right's formidable rejection of the empirical method in favour of a radical and stridently ideological critique. We can focus our attention much more firmly on contemporary cultural conditions, consolidating and developing a continuous analysis of immediately contemporary forms of cultural construction, building on work that has been extensively proposed but only fitfully achieved. We can seek more overt and declarative forms of political consciousness: taking a lead from feminism and stepping out from behind the defensive shield of post-modernist self-consciousness, it may be possible to open up more direct, more confessional, more communicative modes of political dialogue.

Despite the evident theoretical and institutional divergences between 'New Historicism' and cultural materialism, they should still be considered as cognate enterprises, often converging into a strategic synthesis, frequently intermeshing across the ground of a single critical initiative. The task of analysing subsequent, and particularly contemporary, Renaissance reproductions, could scarcely be attempted without the kind of work already performed on the original historical moment of production. What I am advocating here is not a theoretical witch-hunt against New Historicism but rather a different kind of application or strategic mobilisation of finely crafted methodologies already effectively exercised on Renaissance historical materials. I have already emphasised, after Walter Cohen, the desirability of a more open political consciousness, and of a more consistent focus on the present: these seem to me inseparable from any kind of Marxist perspective. In addition I think we should be more willing to approach popular culture: not only the popular culture of the past, the historical institutions of Renaissance carnival, but our own contemporary popular culture of print and image and audio-visual media. If our sphere of cultural attention, even the educational work by means of which we all earn our living, is to be considered in any kind of democratic perspective, we have to recognise that in so far as the majority of people encounter 'the Renaissance' at all, they do so through the media of contemporary popular culture. The material available for comment and analysis in this context is much more extensive than we normally think. To approach it we need, of course, the tools of media study, sociological inquiry and semiotic analysis: many of the comments we have all made, *en passant*, about such phenomena suffer from theoretical naiveté and oversimplification. Our attention should also be focused more broadly on the educational systems as a whole: our work in higher education is not in any except an illusory sense separable from educational practice at all 'levels'.

I am also advocating therefore that as we broaden the focus of our attention to assimilate hitherto neglected materials, so we might also incorporate new and alternative methodologies. Perhaps in the meantime (which brings me back to my starting point) reflecting critically on the ideological implications of some of the methods that have already been established and that seem to be growing into a strange and unforeseen currency.

PART TWO

Culture

CHAPTER THREE

Performance (1985)

✣

1951 WAS THE YEAR in which the post-war Labour government fostered a 'Festival of Britain', intended as a celebration and promotion of British culture coinciding with the centenary of the Great Exhibition of 1851. The purpose underlying the Festival was that of demonstrating the success of the nation's post-war recovery and reconstruction under a Labour administration: to display, in the words of a Board of Trade committee, Britain's 'moral, cultural, spiritual and material' recovery from the destruction and demoralisation of war:

> The main thrust of the Festival was towards advertising British achievements in science, technology and design... but the Festival was a significant cultural phenomenon, both in its conception and its reception. It is interesting to see how literary its treatment was, for the theme, in the words of the official guide, was 'The Autobiography of a Nation'. Those responsible for arranging the various sections of the shows were officially known as script writers, with the exhibition on the South Bank (the centre-piece, but by no means the only piece) divided into chapters of the 'island story'. The literary approach was essentially didactic and propagandist. This was to be 'a challenge to the sloughs of the present and a shaft of confidence cast forth against the future', said the official guide, falling back on the language of the King James' Bible.[1]

The Festival has been described as, to an extent, a continuity from the machinery of war-time propaganda: 'Both in its approach and its selection of personnel, the Festival of Britain betrayed its origins in the efforts and experience of the Ministry of Information and CEMA in wartime, when the idea of theme exhibitions with a confident message was first put into practice.'[2] CEMA, the Council for the Encouragement of Music and the Arts, had been established in 1940 and became the Arts Council in 1946; as an instrument of state patronage its importance had been growing, and it was allocated an extra £400,000 to spend on the Festival itself. But despite the centralised planning, the project was able to build on a very broad basis of national support created by the socialising influences of the war. A broad and active popular participation, familiar enough in traditional rituals such as coronations, jubilees and royal weddings, testified encouragingly to a degree of progress in the direction of a new democratic culture.

In cultural terms, however, the Festival now appears rather as an end to post-war potentialities for progressive change, an anticipation of Winston Churchill's Conservative election victory at the end of the year, than as the symptom of a developing socialist national consciousness. Michael Frayn argued that the Festival testified to the hegemony of a radical middle class, which favoured Labour's programme for achieving social justice provided it was not permitted to change the fundamental basis of British society:

> With the exception of Herbert Morrison, who was responsible to the Cabinet for the Festival and who had very little to do with the actual form it took, there was almost no one of working class background concerned in planning the Festival, and nothing about the results to suggest that the working classes were anything more than the loveable human but essentially inert objects of benevolent administration. In fact Festival Britain was the Britain of the radical middle classes – the do-gooders; the readers of the *New Statesman*, the *Guardian*, and the *Observer*; the signers of petitions; the backbone of the BBC.[3]

Naturally then, this particular 'Autobiography of a Nation' involved, at least in cultural terms, an attempt to establish links with the past rather than a progressive vision of future change. The paradox is visible in the Jacobean language used by the official guide to express future aspiration. The Festival seemed to embody reactionary hopes for re-establishing of past glories rather than a genuinely socialist version of historical progress. Desmond Shaw-Taylor, music critic of the *New Statesman*, articulated precisely (though unintentionally) the contradiction between reactionary aspirations and the harsh economic and social problems those aspirations would leave untouched, using the Shakespeare myth as the proper language of an idealist's vision violated by a sordid contemporary reality:

> I feel as though our Philistine old Albion, so solid and beefy, has turned overnight into Prospero's insubstantial isle; an impression fostered by the strange glamour and glitter of the South Bank. But not for long is Anglo-Saxon reality to be held at bay. Lured on by the novelty and freshness and colour, I drop into one of the Festival restaurants ... and then, ah then, I am soon back in familiar old England. Not indeed in the fine old England of beef sirloins and saddles of mutton, but in our latter-day, take-it-or-leave-it England of lukewarm tomato soup and custard with a skin on the top. [4]

The return to power of Churchill, Shakespearean orator and leader of the 'band of brothers' which saved Britain in her hour of peril, was a fulfilment of those reactionary dreams, visible here in tense contradiction with the progressive hopes of the Labour government's last cultural intervention.

It was therefore entirely predictable that once again 'Shakespeare' should be mobilised to serve the cultural aims of a nationalistic but ostensibly broadly populist and democratic celebration. At this time, before the founding of the Royal Shakespeare Company in 1960, the Shakespeare Memorial Theatre was responsible for running an annual summer season of Shakespeare performances known as the Stratford Summer Festival. As its contribution to the Festival of Britain the Memorial Theatre staged a cycle of the English Histories, the *Richard II-Henry V* tetralogy, integrated into a unified chronological sequence of performances. The ideological context informing the production was the patriotic tradition discussed in the previous chapter, explicitly proclaimed by J. Dover Wilson in an essay called 'Shakespeare and English History as the Elizabethans understood it', contributed to a commemorative volume.[5]

The production represented, Dover Wilson argues, a uniquely successful alliance of criticism and theatre. Both institutions were responsible for distorting and misinterpreting Shakespeare but an effective collaboration of the two would stand a better chance of discovering and fulfilling Shakespeare's 'purposes'. Those 'purposes' found their appropriate medium in the integrated cycle of historical plays, the perfect discourse for an articulation of the Tudor myth. 'Tudor history was entirely, even superstitiously, monarchical … its principal theme was the origin and glorification of the Tudor dynasty.' (p. 7) With unshakeable assurance Dover Wilson asserts that Tudor historiography was entirely monarchical and loyalist and that Shakespeare shared a common purpose with its propagandist motivations. A quotation from G.M. Trevelyan's *History of England* (1926) is employed to demonstrate that only a superstitious and ritualistic monarchism could have sustained the power of the Tudors who evidently ruled by consent rather than force: 'English king-worship', said Trevelyan, 'was the secret of a family and spirit of an age.' This 'brilliant generalisation of our greatest living historian' proves to Dover Wilson 'the amazing fact that the strongest government this country has ever known had literally nothing to back it up – no standing army, no bureaucracy, no police … nothing but the adoration of the people.' (p. 8) Tudor 'Englishmen' looked back over the period of civil wars and rejoiced in the monarchy which had delivered them from the curse providentially imposed for the deposition of Richard II: 'a monarchy divinely ordained, absolute, unchallenged, and entirely popular'. (p. 9) The chief intellectual faith of the age was social order, the great intellectual anxiety fear of social disturbance. Shakespeare's tetralogy follows the pattern of Halle's *Union* and was inspired by the same philosophy of history: the usurpation of Henry IV produced a divinely initiated chaos, an ever-present possibility to the thoughtful Elizabethan, anxious about the succession and unable to conceive of any society but a strong monarchy: 'All that is fundamental, the very stuff of Shakespeare's thought, as it was bound to be in an age when absolute monarchy, legitimacy, and the "divinity that doth hedge a king" seemed the only pillars of the social system.' (p. 9)

The advantage of producing the plays in connected succession was, for Dover Wilson, that the pattern of orthodox Tudor constitutional theory becomes unmistakably clear in dramatic terms as it had already been clarified in criticism and scholarship. The characterisations and perspectives produced by a connected historical narrative would secure more firmly the plays' orthodox moral position. Integration does not complicate the plays' potentiality for generating meaning, but reduces it; the larger and more complex structure does not, paradoxically, open out the plurality of significances but rather constricts them to a fixed, pre-determined frame of reference. There is no possibility, for example, within the whole tetralogy, for an individual actor to develop a role like that of Hotspur or Falstaff to a point where it might introduce a dangerous imbalance into the orthodox moral pattern. Dramatic production of the whole sequence, properly handled, produces, according to Dover Wilson, results identical to those of genuine scholarship and true criticism, by ensuring correct measure and proportion, by eliminating bias and distortion: Bolingbroke and Prince Hal *must* be seen as sympathetic heroes, while Richard II, Hotspur and Falstaff *must* be condemned as forces dangerous to the state:

> As for the notion already glanced at, a notion entertained by many famous critics, that Henry V was a prig and a cad, I make bold to assert that anything so absurd could never have crossed the minds

of either Shakespeare or his audience. To them Henry Monmouth was the ideal representative of order and security … They knew by experience that England's only safeguard against internal strife and 'the envy of less happier lands' was a Prince who, with the sceptre firmly in his grasp, could be the adored leader of a united and harmonious commonwealth, in which noble, merchant, yeoman and peasant worked together for the good of the whole. Such a Prince was their own Queen Elizabeth; such a Prince was Shakespeare's Henry of Monmouth. (p. 22)

Dover Wilson disingenuously describes his contribution to this volume as an attempt to 'supplement with scholarship' the 'findings of the stage'. In fact the production was built on foundations of a pre-existent scholarly and critical orthodoxy, explicitly proclaimed by the Memorial Theatre's Director, Anthony Quayle:

… it seemed to us that the great epic theme of the Histories had become obscured through years of presenting the plays singly, and many false interpretations had grown up, and come to be accepted, through star actors giving almost too persuasive and dominant performances of parts which the author intended to be by no means so sympathetic. Successful theatrical practice over a great number of years had stealthily built a mountain of mis-representation and surrounded it with a fog of ignorance. This was the producers' belief as we worked on the plays, and our purpose in presenting the History Cycle was to rediscover and try to reveal the author's true intentions.[6]

Not surprisingly, the author's true intentions were discovered to be identical with those of Dover Wilson, Tillyard and Wilson Knight: a demonstrative celebration of orthodox Tudor historical thought in which a rigid moral pattern secures a correct apportioning of the audience's 'sympathy': Hal is unquestionably a prodigal prince, ideal king and epic hero; Hotspur simply a hero manqué, Falstaff 'frankly vicious' and ripe for rejection without remorse.

The necessary 'unity' of the productions, as historical chronicle and moralistic parable, prescribed for the producers other kinds of unity: one of which seems to be a genuinely radical shift away from the nineteenth century tradition of spectacular theatre towards a more open dramatic style based on the physical space of the Elizabethan theatre. The set was designed by Tanya Moiseiwitsch to resemble an Elizabethan stage. Anthony Quayle writes:

> The greatest problem was to devise a single setting which could serve all four plays, for to have invented different settings for each play would have destroyed that very unity for which we were striving, that unity which Shakespeare's own Globe preserved so well. The set had to be capable of embracing court and tavern, shire and city, indoor and out-of-door; it had to be the lists at Coventry and the quay-side at Southampton; it had to house the rebels in their barn before the battle of Shrewsbury, and the dying Bolingbroke in the Jerusalem chamber; and, since this list must have an end, it had to suggest the 'wooden O' of *Henry V.* (p. ix)

The set was constructed behind the proscenium arch and centred around a large wooden structure with a double-door entrance at stage level, a railed platform above and flights of stairs leading down on each side. A throne stood by the proscenium arch as a permanent feature; otherwise props and hangings were introduced to suggest different locations – a palace, a garden, an inn, a battlefield. Behind the central structure was a cyclorama, illuminated to simulate sky for exterior locations, darkened or covered by hangings for indoor scenes. Despite the obvious modifications, the set's resemblance to an Elizabethan stage is readily apparent and was evidently accepted as such by a range of critical judgements. The volume quotes one from the *Sunday Times* which suggests that this production improved on the Elizabethan theatre:

> This year at Stratford (for the first time as far as I know) there has been a real attempt to stage the history plays as Shakespeare intended them to be staged, while avoiding any painful sense of pedantic archaism. Tanya Moiseiwitsch's permanent set was not a reconstruction of the Globe Theatre, but an improvement on it. By using steps up to a wide gallery, with doors opening out under-

neath it, the set had all the variety of Upper, Lower and Inner Stage which the plays demand, but without the limitation of movement between which was obviously an undesirable feature of the Globe.[7]

T.A. Jackson writing in the communist *Daily Worker* offered the same proposition with enthusiastic acceptance:

> Let me say at once that the performance was very fine. The stage setting reproduced admirably the lay-out of the stage of Shakespeare's day and so made possible all the pageantry business without any of that over lavish gorgeousness deemed imperative on the flat stage of Beerbohm Tree and Henry Irving. The pageantry and grouping were well designed and perfectly rehearsed; the actors played as a team – nobody trying to steal the picture from anybody else.[8]

To this left-wing critic the production combined a number of favourable features: a noticeable taming-down of the gorgeous pageantry previously regarded as inseparable from Shakespeare's histories in performance; the construction of an emblematic rather than an illusionistic set, with the flexibility and openness of the Elizabethan stage and the prevalence of ensemble performance over the star system. In their context these initiatives were obviously to a degree progressive. They certainly throw light on the subsequent development of the RSC which was clearly, in a limited sense, a force of progressive cultural change.[9] Perhaps this production was mobilising a new Shakespeare: the appropriate contribution to a cultural festival which was, at least theoretically, based upon the popular successes of the Labour government in laying the foundations for a potentially progressive and democratic national unity.

The apparently radical initiative embodied in the set – the one aspect of the production, apart from Michael Redgrave's expressionistic acting, to receive serious criticism – proves on closer inspection to have been too firmly meshed in the institutional and ideological character of the Shakespeare Memorial Theatre itself, and too strictly controlled by the orthodoxy which

formed the production's intellectual credentials, to progress very
far towards a radical new Shakespeare. The permanent set was
conceived as an inclusive element in an overall 'continuity', an
ideology of unified totality, which posed impervious barriers to
the liberation of Shakespearean performance:

> Continuity is the essence of the presentation, and three conditions
> are necessary to achieve it. First, a controlling director who can fit
> the four productions into his conception. Then a permanent set
> which remains unchanged throughout, to give us the illusion of
> unity of place. Thirdly, a set of actors who can carry from play to
> play those roles which overlap: and this not just in the major roles,
> Bolingbroke, Hal, Falstaff, but no less in the subsidiary parts,
> Northumberland, Westmorland, Lady Percy, and the characters
> from low life.[10]

The first requirement flows naturally from the play's ideological
basis: a 'controlling director' committed to an orthodox critical
interpretation would police the production, ensuring a consistent
loyalty and adherence to a predetermined ideological pattern.
The second stipulation reveals that the function of the permanent set was dependent on an uncritical commitment to illusionistic dramatic representation. This was also the distinctive
character of the acting, as the illustrative still photographs and
the unperturbed pleasure of the theatre critics quoted in the
commemorative volume both illustrate, and of the costumes
and armour, reflecting an attempt at illusionistic historical
reconstruction. The third point testifies to the dominance of
naturalism over the theatrical freedom of Elizabethan dramatic
conventions: though minor parts were doubled, and Redgrave
assigned several star characters, the major roles were sustained
by consistent castings, thus naturalising an actor in a particular
part.

The distance between the style of this production and the
radical potentialities of the Elizabethan theatre is now more
visible, and can be used to measure accurately the production's
conservative character. The stage set was much more illusionistic

than an Elizabethan stage: distinguishing place and time by artificial lighting and by extensive embellishment and decoration (in
the final scene of *Henry V* the whole stage was transformed by
elaborate hangings and canopies into a naturalistic interior representing the French court).[11] In the Elizabethan theatre, time and
place had to be signalled by convention so that both would always
remain flexible and relative. The audience would always sustain
an awareness of the constructed artifice of the proceedings and
would never be seduced into the oblivion of empathetic illusion.
Though an audience accustomed to the pageant and panoply of
pre-war Shakespeare productions would doubtless find the stage
forbidding and austere, there was no encouragement to the audience to recognise it as a stage, the conventionally signified site of
a simulated reality. The Shakespeare Memorial Theatre could not
but remain a nineteenth century theatre, with a proscenium-arch
stage that constituted the performance as a partitioned representation of reality, and the audience as remote and passive observers
'reading', rather than experiencing or participating in the performance. The Elizabethan stage depended on an entirely different relationship between actors and audience, with the spectators
crowded on three (possibly four) sides, their visible and tangible
presence exerting a far more distinct pressure on the nature of the
production.[12]

The 1951 Festival production was thus able to hand the Dover
Wilson/Tillyard/Wilson Knight version of Tudor ideology wholesale, to a passive audience, as a complete and unquestionable
totality stripped of all its internal contradictions and constitutive
tensions. As the stage becomes more naturalistic, it becomes
more authoritarian and more effective in allowing ideology a free
and unhampered passage to the spectator. As the stage becomes
more illusionistic, it permits less space for the collaborative
creation of meaning natural to the Elizabethan theatre. As
the audience is further removed from the action, it becomes
a passive consumer of a fixed ideology rather than an active
constituency intensely involved in a complex process of recipro-

cal communication in which ideologies can be interrogated, contradictions made visible, conventions subverted and orthodoxies exposed.

By contrast Jane Howell's 1983 television production[13] of the 'first tetralogy' of English History plays – *Henry VI Parts One, Two and Three,* and *Richard III* – can be taken as a striking example of the radical potentialities of Shakespeare in performance (particularly striking in the context of an overwhelmingly orthodox series such as the *BBC-TV Shakespeare*). The radical energies of the drama were released in part by a conscious attempt to reconstruct some of the physical characteristics of Elizabethan and pre-Tudor theatre: not by using a reconstructed model of a Renaissance playhouse, which would not adapt to film treatment, but by devising a set, a production style and an acting convention which would perform some of the functions of the Elizabethan theatre without denying the contemporaneity of the performance. I have considered the aesthetic and ideological effects of a production designed to convey historical authenticity, both by its echoes of the Elizabethan stage and its effort to construct a historically convincing simulacrum of fifteenth century reality. The privileging of historical authenticity, in Shakespeare's time a progressive force, has become in our own century a conservative one. While the emergent class of Tudor England sought a vision of real historical process to challenge Christian providentialism, for us that positivistic science of history has become pre-eminently the history of our own ruling class. In terms of dramatic production, the locking of a play into a definite and finished historical period by costume, mise en scène and acting styles can now be seen as a systematic resistance to change rather than a recognition of its inevitability. We must require of historical drama the potentiality for alienating and reflecting on its own constructed reality as well as the embodiment, in that constructed reality, of a historiographical interpretation.

Jane Howell's production needs to be considered in juxtaposition with the BBC's version of the second tetralogy, broadcast in

1978 and 1979, a relationship of contrast that I have discussed
more thoroughly elsewhere.[14] The *Richard II-Henry V* cycle was
directed by David Giles under the producership of Cedric Messina: the productions are a fair sample of orthodox, establishment
Shakespeare, endemic to the BBC-TV series. The decision of
Cedric Messina to make the English histories a basic constituent
of the first two 'seasons' was correctly diagnosed by an American
reviewer as an act of chauvinism, locating the *BBC-TV Shakespeare* in a tradition of British national drama.

> In the first two 'seasons' (1978–9) ... there has been a clear empha-
> sis on British history – almost half the plays ... Cedric Messina,
> the originator of the series and the producer of the first two sea-
> sons ... thinks the histories, from *Richard II* up to *Henry V*, are
> "the highest achievement of Shakespeare's art ... It seems to me,
> with a lot of hindsight, that these histories are a sort of "Curse of
> the House of Atreus in English" ... *Richard II, 1 and 2 Henry IV*
> and *Henry V* ... work out a cycle of guilt, retribution and expia-
> tion for the murder of *Richard II*. The BBC productions are very
> conscious of the continuities of this cycle'.[15]

The overall conception of these plays is correctly diagnosed here
as the conventional Tillyard doctrine of providential order violated by usurpation, providential retribution punishing the guilty.
The traditionalist line was confirmed and supported by right-
wing theoretician Paul Johnson who contributed an associated
broadcast:

> According to the orthodox Tudor view of history, the deposition
> of the rightful and anointed king, Richard II, was a crime against
> God, which thereafter had to be expiated by the nation in a series
> of bloody struggles ... Shakespeare found in the tragic circum-
> stances of Richard II's life a very clear illustration of the general
> principle that the rule of law was the only barrier against anarchy.
> Every man in society, in his proper place and degree had rights
> and duties ... Hierarchy was ordained by divine justice and
> human law.[16]

Television production obviously made much more readily available possibilities for organising the plays into an integrated historical narrative:

> It was decided that the English histories, from Richard II through the *Henry IV's, V* and *VI* to *Richard III*, would be presented in chronological order so that some day in the not too distant future, the eight plays that form this sequence will be able to be seen in their historical order, a unique record of the chronicled history of that time.[17]

Messina's global ambition was fulfilled, but not as he originally envisaged its realisation. Far from securing a uniformity and continuity of style for the whole cycle, the BBC permitted Jane Howell to mount a production which thoroughly subverted the ideological stability of the earlier versions. The second tetralogy emerges from this production as a constituent element in an inclusive and integrated dramatic totality, illustrating the violation of natural social 'order' by the deposition of a legitimate king. The plays are produced in 'classic drama' style with predominantly naturalistic devices of acting, *mise en scène* and filming. Actors are identified wholly with their roles, growing old in them; settings are more naturalistic than conventionalised; camera movements and angles always 'straightforward' with no 'arty-craft' shooting.

In the case of Jane Howell's production of the first historical tetralogy, the director's whole conception of the Shakespearean history play diverges strikingly from that propounded by Cedric Messina and evidently accepted by David Giles. Where Messina saw the history plays conventionally as orthodox Tudor historiography, and the director employed dramatic techniques which allow that ideology a free and unhampered passage to the spectator, Jane Howell takes a more complex view of the first tetralogy as, simultaneously, a serious attempt at historical interpretation and as a drama with a peculiarly modern relevance and contemporary application. The director's conception of the plays emphasised their revelation of historical change: not the 'mutability' which operates within a framework of universal order, nor the meaningless flux of metaphysical historicism, but the collision of institutions and ideologies within a specific historical formation. In this case the dialectic of chivalry dissolves from a precarious code of social order into ruthless competition for power: a historical situation which cannot be identified with, but can indirectly suggest, analogies with the present:

> ... the code of the people had been for a long time a belief in chivalry; in the first play one starts to see the death of chivalry, which was epitomised in *Henry V* ... When times change people don't realise it for an awfully long time, and so one still has the remnants of chivalry in many ways in Part Two ... with Gloucester's death anarchy is loosed ... You're into a time of change in which there is no code except survival of the fittest ... what interests me is that I think we are today in that sort of state, in a time of change.[18]

At the same time there was no intention of sealing the plays firmly into a remote historical period visible only as colourful pageant. By securing a link with perennial traditions of popular entertainment, the production team hoped to synthesise the historical and the contemporary into a single complex dimension capable of generating multiplicity of meaning. The set designer, Oliver Bayldon, recorded that the set was based on an adventure playground in Fulham, south-west London: ' ... it really was very medieval: it had nooses and cross beams and a bit like a tower: ...' With a power station looming in the background the location suggested 'equally images of modernity and shadows of medieval castle'. 'We talked about medieval scale and the idea of a circus ... then the mystery play's stages became the towers we now have ... We'd talked about Northern Ireland and Beirut and South America, warlords and factions, and I'd been trying to make it as modern as possible, yet at the same time not modern in such a way that it distracts.'[19]

Howell's ambition was partially to respect those specific characteristics inscribed in the play by the material conditions of its original production: the plays could be made to function as they

originally did only by restoring them to a similar physical environment:

> ... because I knew Shakespeare had written for a company, and
> you can sense in the plays that there's a lot of doubling, you just
> know that his company was fifteen or perhaps it was augmented
> to twenty-five, so there must have been a lot of doubling again. I
> felt: Go back to the original rules. It just seemed practically *and*
> artistically a good idea. I was very concerned with obeying the
> original rules of the play. I think if you're going to do a play you'd
> better know how it was done originally ... because it will only
> work on a certain sort of structure.[20]

Howell evidently managed to establish for the production something like an Elizabethan *ensemble*, very different from the star-
system operating in the earlier production of the second
tetralogy:

> With this sequence of four plays Howell has once again, as is both
> her habit and her policy, brought together a group of actors many
> of whom she has worked with before ... who form her unofficial
> repertory company.[21]

Like an Elizabethan stage, the set was deliberately designed as
non-representational and unlocalised. Sir Philip Sidney would
have bitterly resented the arbitrary flexibility of a single space
designated as a court, a castle, a garden, a battlefield, purely by
signalled convention. The combination of a non-illusionistic set
and actors doubling roles prevents any possibility of a complete
'suspension of disbelief' on the part of the audience. The acting
styles too, though enormously varied, were based on a rejection
of Stanislavskian method:

> Shakespeare you have to say and allow to affect you rather than
> seeking to justify the lines. A lot of the work is to say, 'Look, what
> is the line, what is the intellectual sense, *play* the intellectual sense,
> stop mucking about with the emotions, follow the intellect'. You
> have to go that way round rather than doing all this method non-
> sense – which none of my lot do anyway – of getting yourself in a
> state and then going on to play it.[22]

Evidently the producer Jonathan Miller's personal influence over this production was minimal, and one can gather probable reasons for this. Asked in an interview how one should stage battle-scenes for the TV screen, he replied that any form of stylisation or theatrical presentation would have to be compatible with the irrepressible realism of the camera's mode of perception; various devices could be employed, but 'one would hesitate to use them in the really important plays ... since they seem to take place in the less good plays, the introduction of electronic gimmickry could be an aid to covering up a second-rate play ... '[23] The producer's withdrawal of interest from these self-evidently 'second-rate' plays obviously created a space for the creative intervention of a genuinely radical director. She solved the problem of battle-scenes simply by using film techniques, montage and rapid cutting. The climatic battle of *Henry VI Part One* was 'carefully scored as a transition in terms of style', beginning with a self-evidently theatrical, staged fight, filmed in long-shots; modulating into a filmic 'montage of very quick details ... tight, fast and hard' and returning to the naturalist/theatrical mode for a static close-up vision of Talbot's death. The director's willingness to embrace the theatrical, to mix conventions and to violate naturalism enabled her to make strikingly effective television of material declared by the Executive Producer to be practically unscreenable. A theatricalised historical pageant presents the spectator with a dramatising of history in which the history is less prominent than the dramatisation. A filmic montage conveys by a 'theatre of cruelty' assault on the senses the bloody savagery of a historic civil war, applicable to any war in any time and place. The ideology of chivalry is interrogated from a liberal-individualist perspective by the intense *personalising* of Talbot's dying speech, naturalistically played and filmed in a moving and gory close-up.

This production illustrates effectively how the theatrical style hinted at by the 1951 production could be pushed much further towards a radical reproduction of Shakespeare's historiography. The set was completely non-illusionistic, looking both modern and Elizabethan and pretending to be neither. Costumes were a mixture of the historical and the emblematic. Acting styles varied but with a general avoidance of straight forward naturalism: the alienating device of direct address to camera was used extensively. Jonathan Miller is quoted as arguing that it would be impossible to mix the conventions of television with those of an Elizabethan theatre – hopeless to try recreating the 'wooden O' within the 'electronic square'.[24] His primary concern here was, as always, to defend television naturalism but he makes a persuasive point about television's elimination of the audience. How could the live audience of an Elizabethan play be contained within the television screen's frame? Jane Howell solved this problem simply by constituting members of the cast, as frequently as possible, as an active and participating audience, bringing the vitality and changeableness of that audience to the customary blankness of the television screen.

Here then are two examples of 'history in performance', both in their way experimental, both attempting to establish a continuity with the Elizabethan theatre. To express in a concise formula the distinctions between the divergent kinds of drama produced by these different versions of Shakespeare's history plays, we could do worse than adopt Brecht's distinction between 'Theatre for Pleasure' and 'Theatre for Instruction', between the drama of empathy and the drama of 'alienation'.

> The dramatic theatre's spectator says: Yes, I have felt like that too – Just like me – it's only natural – It'll never change – The sufferings of this man appal me, because they are inescapable – That's great art; it all seems the most obvious thing in the world – I weep when they weep, I laugh when they laugh.
>
>   The epic theatre's spectator says: I'd never have thought it – That's not the way – That's extraordinary, hardly believable – It's got to stop – The sufferings of this man appal me, because they are unnecessary – That's great art: nothing obvious in it – I laugh when they weep, I weep when they laugh.[25]

The Elizabethan theatre was not a theatre of illusion. It was rather a theatre of alienation, in the sense familiarised by the dramatic theory and practice of Brecht. A theatre audience watching a modern-dress production of a Shakespeare play in one of our 'national' theatres, though conscious of some tension between language and visual style, will assume that the play is addressed primarily to the present. A television audience watching David Giles' BBC production of *Henry IV*, which operates entirely in the conventions of television naturalism (in terms of which a studio set, for example, appears naturalised and not instantly recognisable as a wooden construction) will gather that the play is about the fifteenth century. Both audiences are responding to, and have their perceptions constituted by, aesthetic conventions of an illusionistic kind, which insist on the *reality* of the illusion they convey, their own fictionality. But the Elizabethan stage was neither naturalistic nor illusionistic. Modern costume was a neutral accompaniment of a familiar modern environment and a contemporary, though highly specialised, language: it did not distract the audience from appreciating the historical world signified in a particular style of poetry, such as the language of chivalry in Richard II. Moreover, the stage being unlocalised, times could be distinguished or identified as easily as places. If, as Sidney complained, you could have Asia on one side of the stage and Africa on another, so on the same stage the fifteenth century could co-exist with the present. A chivalric medieval prince could meet a band of sixteenth century soldiers led by a figure from immemorial carnival, as happens in *Henry IV, Part Two*. But co-existence is not confusion in a theatre of alienation: the distinctions between time and place can be held as easily as the distinctions between actor and role, between visible object and signified fiction, between empathic identification and detached objective interest.

History on the Elizabethan stage was not merely a mirror of the contemporary world, nor was it simply a historical reconstruction of the past. A historical play in the Elizabethan theatre was (like all Elizabethan plays) a complex montage capable of connecting and distinguishing diverse realities, past and present time, near and remote space, subjective consciousness and exterior world. The past could be perceived as past, not to be confused with the present, and yet capable of relevance to the present by the exercise of the curious metaphorical imagination typical of Renaissance thought. Shakespeare's relationship with the past was one of knowledge through difference.

CHAPTER FOUR

National Culture (1991)

✿

I N THE *DAILY MAIL* of 29 March 1984, Jack Tinker reviewed a production of *Henry V*:

Offhand, I can't remember a day when it seemed so marvellous or mad to be English. Suddenly the chronic inconvenience of London's transport strike and the continuing horrors of the mining dispute were put into the merciful perspective of history.

It began in Westminster Abbey where I sat close to the Queen Mother and watched her fight back tears and surrender to smiles with a packed congregation as the funniest hours of her reign were celebrated in the familiar words and music of Sir Noel Coward.

And it ended here at Stratford, with a young, brave and poetic Henry bridging the centuries between by reminding us of the unlikely spirit which won Agincourt. Nothing much seemed so very different ...

What links the vision of young Mr Kenneth Branagh, making his Royal Shakespeare debut as a raw, stocky warrior, with Coward's latterday musings, is the patriotic poet which lurked beneath their different facades ...

To hear Mr Branagh wonder incredulously at the valour of his rag-tag-and-bobtail troops was to hear echoes of Derek Jacobi reading the moving war diaries of Coward at the unveiling of his memorial stone.

And when Branagh squats among his men, blackened with the efforts of war, and urges them once more into the breach –

well, we had heard that sentiment back in the Abbey when Penelope Keith set the sea of handkerchiefs dabbing at moist eyes ...

I won't press the coincidence. Suffice to say that neither the
service at the Abbey nor Adrian Noble's spare, bare production
at Stratford were mere tub-thumping exercises in mindless
nationalism.

There was pain, irony, wit and humanity in both. As Ian
McDairmid's conversational chorus informs us: Henry had a
kingdom for a stage. Which of course was like Coward turning his
stage into a kingdom. Both, in their way make a little thing like a
transport shut-down seem irrelevant. All this from old masters
and new blood! Between Harry's Harfleur spirit and Coward's
London Pride, it did not, after all, seem improbable that there are
still good reasons to be in England now that April's almost here.[1]

The distinction here between 'patriotism' (of the handkerchief-
dabbing type) and 'nationalism' (of the tub-thumping variety) is
a reasonable starting point for the following explorations of
British patriotic and national identities, as they appear mediated
through the cultural reproduction of Shakespearean drama, and
in particular through Kenneth Branagh's widely celebrated film
adaptation of *Henry V*, itself based on the 1984 Royal Shakespeare
Company stage production eulogised in Jack Tinker's review.[2] To
have a forceful and vigorous ideology of nationalism, you have to
have a forceful and vigorous nation to enact and substantiate it. If
the 'nation' in question happens, like Britain, to be an eclipsed
world power – no longer a great imperial aggressor, no longer a
significant colonial leader, no longer a dominant industrial or
economic force – then what basis remains for a particular, quan-
tifiable 'national' consciousness? If the political and economic
character of the 'nation' owes more to its participation in larger
political and economic units – the EEC, NATO, American foreign
policy, the multinational capitalist economy, the International
Monetary Fund – then what sense does it make to continue talk-
ing about a specific, isolable 'national' identity?

All that seems left to the disappointed or reformed British
nationalist is an emotion of 'patriotism', which can evidently be

distinguished from the politics of nationalism, and is capable of surviving such losses and transformations as the demise of Empire and the descent from world eminence relatively undamaged and unscathed. Patriotism is associated with 'poetry', with emotion, with the heart, with tears; 'nationalism' with 'mindless' aggression, with 'tub-thumping' jingoistic assertiveness. In a review of the subsequent film version of *Henry V*, Tom Hutchinson in the *Mail on Sunday* later proposed the same distinction: 'the film ... touches the heart of emotion rather than the instinct for patriotism'.[3] But in the earlier review of the stage production, patriotism is indissolubly linked with the past. The plangency of patriotic feeling here derives from what Tom Nairn calls 'the glamour of backwardness': a nostalgia, a craving, unappeasable hunger for that which is irretrievably lost. Yet that loss may be regarded also as neither complete nor inconsolable, since the utterances of a 'patriotic poet' such as William Shakespeare (or Noel Coward) can transcend the absence and negation of history, and suffuse the soul with – not exactly a new fulfilment but at least a new longing – a new mixing of memory and desire. Militaristic violence, inseparable from the historical actuality of nationalism, is strangely appeased in this flood of remembrance,[4] strangely pacified by 'the merciful perspective of history'. The British patriot, now no longer a nationalist, looks back regretfully, with resigned sadness, to his 'finest hour' in 1940, or the 'unlikely' victory of his ancestors at Agincourt; but, as re-awakened memories, these scenes of historical violence, recollected in tranquillity, acquire a power to comfort and console.

The patriotic emotion is anchored in the past. Inspired by the 'valour', 'gallantry' and 'courage' displayed by the manly deeds of a warrior race, and immortalised in the words of the 'old masters' (represented here by the in-this-context-unfortunately-named 'Shake-spear' and 'Coward'), patriotism paradoxically expresses itself in gestures of weakness, in a 'surrender' to tears. The binary polarisation of gender implicit in this construction is evident in the femininity shared by those cast, respectively, as tear-jerker and tear-jerked (Penelope Keith and the Queen Mother). The contradictory quality of the patriotic emotion itself is manifested in the male observer's luxurious relishing of a weakness discovered in the contemplation of strength – like D.H. Lawrence, the writer here enjoys feeling his 'manhood cast / Down in the flood of remembrance' as he 'weeps like a child for the past.'[5]

The patriotic emotion is anchored in the past, and besieged, embattled in the present. The England that surrounds Jack Tinker gives him no cause for patriotic celebration: it is rather a scene of bitter social conflict and class-antagonism, an England of transport and coalfield strikes. The English patriot doesn't see his emotional conviction rooted in the actuality of the nation that surrounds him which seems systematically to negate his ideal national image. The patriotic emotion searches past and future for a habitable space, nostalgically embracing the glamour of backwardness, and optimistically extrapolating a projected landscape of hope. Elsewhere in the review Tinker quotes some lines from Noel Coward's *Cavalcade* that exactly encapsulate that contradictory emotion:

> Let's drink to the spirit of gallantry and courage that made a strange Heaven out of unbelievable Hell, and let's drink to the Hope, that one day this country of ours, which we love so much, will find dignity and greatness and peace again.

✧

The authentic accent of what might anachronistically be described as a 'post-modern' patriotism can be located in what we think of as the very heart of the traditional discourse of British nationalism: it is even there in that notorious speech attributed to John of Gaunt in Shakespeare's *Richard II*, which in turn provided subsequent ages with a basic vocabulary of patriotic rhetoric.

> This royal throne of kings, this sceptred isle
> This earth of majesty, this seat of Mars,
> This other Eden, demi-paradise,
> This fortress built by Nature for herself
> Against infection and the hand of war,
> This happy breed of men, this little world,
> This precious stone set in a silver sea
> Which serves it in the office of a wall
> Or as a moat defensive to a house
> Against the envy of less happier lands,
> This blessed plot, this earth, this realm, this England ...
>
> (*Richard II*, II.i.40–50)

It is natural to think of this fictionalised John of Gaunt as a great supporter of monarchical prerogative and royal power: certainly outside the play his famous patriotic speech has invariably been employed to endorse absolute authority, to support the autocratic will of many subsequent British kings and governments. Within the play, of course, this speech actually functions as a diatribe of criticism against the ruling monarch: Gaunt is not even depicting the England of the present but expressing a nostalgic regret for an England which has long since vanished into the historical past. It is precisely because the England he sees before him – Richard's England – falls so far short of his idealised vision of what he believes England once was, that his poetic vision of national glory is so brightly and vividly imagined.

The realm of England is here defined largely in terms of its monarchy, its history distinguished by the quality of its kings: but the monarchs Gaunt idealises are not like Richard. They are the warlike, crusading, feudal kings of the early Middle Ages: so Gaunt's speech is after all no panegyric of royal absolutism but a lament for the passing of a feudal kingdom in which king and nobility were united by a natural balance of forces into a 'happy breed of men'. Gaunt's speech is not merely an appeal for strong leadership in the king and it is certainly not a defence of the Renaissance doctrine of divine right and absolute royal authority. On the contrary, he imagines royal authority as inseparable from the power of the nobility; the golden age he longs for and regrets is that of a feudalism held together by the authority of a strong king and by the power of a strong aristocracy. Gaunt's attack on Richard's style of government concentrates on the fact that Richard has replaced the feudal bonds of 'fealty' – the system of reciprocal obligations which bind lord and subject in a feudal polity – with economic contracts:

> England, bound in with the triumphant sea ...
> ... is now bound in with shame,
> With inky blots and rotten parchment bonds
> (II.i.63–4)

Richard is now a mere 'landlord' of England, rather than a king; he has sought to dispense with the loyal co-operation of the nobility and to rule with the assistance of an upstart bureaucracy of 'favourites'. Determined to shake off the influence of the barons, he has introduced radical economic policies to raise revenue without reliance on the great landholders. The unacceptability of Richard's kingship consists, in Gaunt's eyes, in his modernising programme of de-feudalisation, and his consequent slighting of the traditional aristocracy. It is ironic that so many subsequent appeals to English patriotism have been mounted on the basis of this elegant and barbaric statement of baronial self-interest, this celebration of a class that has scarcely earned the unqualified admiration of even the most conservative of thinkers. But as we shall see, this hypostatisation of a sectional class-interest as the ideology of a 'nation' is a symptomatic element in the history of British patriotism.

When the patriotic rhetoric of this speech is imitated, Gaunt's investment in the glamour of backwardness is often incorporated along with the imperious vigour of his nationalistic vision. Some years ago the Department of the Environment produced a television advertisement as part of an anti-litter campaign. A succession of visual images depicted urban squalor, industrial detritus and general untidiness – a river sweating oil and tar; empty streets blowing with waste paper like tumbleweed in a Western ghost-town; a cat snarling in a filthy gutter outside the idly flap-ping doors of a pub. The images were accompanied by those famous and familiar Shakespearean lines, spoken in voice-over commentary. Lines we are accustomed to hear uttered with a hush of reverence and breathless adoration, and with a musical effect akin to the sound of the last post being played at sunset across some colonial parade ground in the Far East, were here intoned harshly, with an accent of resentment, bitterness, and dissatisfaction. Gaunt's patriotic speech was made to operate as an aggrieved, harshly ironic commentary on the scenes of depressing untidiness. At some time, the voice implied, things have been different; Britain was once a proud (and tidy) nation; this royal throne of Kings had not always been so besmirched and soiled by – litter; there was a time when the seat of Mars was cleaned regularly, and when this other Eden was genuinely fit for human habitation.

A moment's consideration of the standards of civic hygiene prevalent in the 1590s would provoke some scepticism about this implicit claim. The advertisement, however, had little use for authentic historical difference, being concerned only to con-struct, through the language of Shakespeare, an ideal type of 'the English nation', against which image the shortcomings of the present might be measured. Its persuasive discourse was no sim-ple reproof, admonishment or rational appeal, but rather a pater-nalistic rebuke, a constituting of the untidy British subject as a violator of purity and innocence, guilty of profaning an idealised image of what the nation once was, and might be again. Think, intones the Shakespearean voice, think of the august and distin-guished company of ancestral illuminati, ancient and modern, you are offending by your anti-social behaviour: those celebrated knights of the theatre like Sir Laurence Olivier and Sir John Giel-gud, with whom such speeches are customarily associated; their great chivalric grandsires, that earlier generation of militaristic rather than histrionic knights, such as John of Gaunt; various kings and queens, ancient and modern, sometimes rulers of 'this sceptred isle'; and above all their heir, the modern custodian of this precious stone, set in a silver sea – Mrs Thatcher, the national housekeeper Herself. Thus a text which was originally the expression of an inconsolable nostalgia for another time, is mobilised as an authoritative voie enjoining on us all an active commitment to the glamour of backwardness. The nostalgic lament for a vanished Elizabethan age takes us spiralling vertiginously down the intertextual labyrinths of quotation, with no terminus in sight, this side of Paradise, other than a fourth term of Tory government.

❧

We began in Westminster Abbey, that focal point of traditional 'British' culture where the institutions of church, monarchy, and democratic constitution (in Philip Larkin's words) 'meet, blend and are robed as destinies'.[6] With imagined wing our swift scene now flies, via John of Gaunt's image of England as a 'precious stone set in a silver sea', to a margin, an edge, a border; to the south coast of Britain, and specifically to those white cliffs of Dover, over which, in Vera Lynn's wartime song, 'there will be blue-birds' – 'tomorrow, just you wait and see'. What more lyrical expression could there be of the patriotic hunger for an endlessly deferred fulfilment than that poignant expression of elegiac existentialism which, like John of Gaunt's speech, and Noel Coward's *Cavalcade*, attaches its emotion to the past and future as a way of confronting the absence and pain of the present? The iconic image that goes with the song is, of course, the famous white cliffs themselves, that long chalk escarpment which offers to the envy of less happier lands so characteristically 'English' a seascape.

'Wherefore to *Dover*?' my reader might well enquire, echoing the accumulating incredulities of Regan and Cornwall in *King Lear*. 'Wherefore to Dover? The seaport of Dover, those famous white cliffs, and more generally the stretch of coastline from Southampton to the Thames estuary, occupy a peculiar and privileged place in the iconography and mythology of British nationalism. My initial reference to Vera Lynn invokes the Second World War, and specifically the period 1940–4 when France was under German occupation, and Britain in constant fear of an invasion. That 'rump' of England then felt (not for the first time) the vulnerability of exposure to another land-mass, the threatening point of France that pokes aggressively towards southern Britain, intimately close in space (narrow enough to swim across) yet always mistrusted, perpetually perceived as alien, frequently feared. Of course, in a war of aerial transport, long-range heavy bombers, guided missiles, that part of England was (though subject to shelling from the French coast) in many ways no more vulnerable than any other, its borders capable of being breached at any point. But it is those cliffs of the south coast that provide us with our most characteristic national image of vulnerability, exposure, openness to the peril of foreign invasion.

The mythological status of the white cliffs of Dover is far more ancient than 1940. In those legendary and mythological narratives that preceded the advent of modern historiography, Dover was actually what the anthropologist Malinowski called a 'spot of origins', a particular geographical location regarded by tradition as the source of a nation's genesis. Anthropologists have identified in the proliferation of such narratives a structural form which they term the 'myth of origin', a narrative which purports to explain the process of a nation's appearance in history. Medieval historians traced the ancestry of their various national populations and monarchies to the dispersal of the Trojan princes after the fall of Troy and Geoffrey of Monmouth claimed that the English were descended from Brutus, allegedly a descendant of Aeneas. In Holinshed there is a narrative describing the conquest of what was to become Britain by Brutus, whose companion Corineus succeeded in overthrowing the giant Gogmagog, the island's original inhabitant 'by reason whereof the place was named long after, *The Fall or leape of Gogmagog*, but afterwards it was called *The Fall of Dover*'.[7] As John Turner has shown, such pseudo-historical narratives were retold in the Renaissance as morality fables, calculated to guide political conduct but they were also retold as myths, designed to legitimise power: 'The black holes in time were to be occluded, the dangerous discontinuities of history papered over with myths that would confirm authority and marginalise the claims of political opposition.'[8] When James I in 1604 had himself proclaimed King of 'Great Britain', he was deliberately re-introducing an antiquarian geographical term in order to establish 'one single rule' over England and Scotland. The name itself was falsely derived from Brutus, and in 1605 James was celebrated in the Lord Mayor's show as the second Brutus who, in fulfilment of Merlin's ancient prophecy, would 'reunite what the original Brutus had put asunder'.[9]

The narratives of this 'mythical charter' enact a sequence of invasion, conquest, colonisation and fragmenting. Dover is the point of entry, the aperture through which a new force of domination can enter the territory, settle it, and then – in a tragic political error – part it asunder. Reading through the political to the sexual, Britain is the female body, invaded by the colonising male; the appropriate feminine resistance is overthrown and the country planted with fertile seed. The inevitable result of this process is however not unity, but parturition, splitting, division; not the formation of a single unified whole but the multiplying of centrifugal energies. The myth imagines national origin as a cyclical process of invasion, unification, plantation and division.

Precisely because in this myth Dover is the source of national identity, it is also the weakest point of the territory's physical defences. What one male can do to a female body, what one conqueror can do to a territory, another male, another conqueror, can repeat and in every repetition the action is (in an important sense) identical. The fundamentally unitary nature of conquest/ intercourse cuts sharply across powerful taboos based on binary oppositions of difference (legitimate/illegitimate, married/ unmarried, pure/contaminated, good/evil) and thereby forms the basis of that male sexual jealousy which in turn butts onto xenophobic nationalism: that point where the linked elements of 'father' and 'fatherland' in the word 'patriotism' meet. Along the south coast England presents her white, chaste purity to the potential invader as a defensive repellent but also as a temptation. 'Succeed where Napoleon failed' urges an advertisement for the local south-east England tourist industry, the words emblazoned across an aerial photograph of the familiar iconic escarpment: 'spend a day in White Cliffs country'. The point where the nation's identity begins is also the point where it could most easily be violated or re-conquered.[10]

❖

A key scene of Shakespeare's *Henry V* (Act II, scene ii) is set on that coastline, historically at Southampton (though usefully, for my purposes, the Folio text of the play misprints Southampton as 'Dover'). Henry and his nobles have here reached the 'extreme verge' of their territorial confine, a point of no return. Everything has been staked on the success of the French adventure; at the end of the scene Henry affirms, rhetorically but accurately, that his authority as monarch depends on victory: 'No King of England, if not King of France'. At this margin of the kingdom, which has the perilous quality of all territorial borders, the riskiest, most uneven odds at Agincourt – is encountered: internal dissension, mutiny within the ranks, self-betrayal. The periphery of England, that no-man's-land between England and France, marked by the sharp dividing line of the white cliffs, sanctified by the legendary myth of origins, is the point chosen for the enactment of a particular ritual: the cleansing of the English body politic by a sacrificial execution.

In the play-text Exeter defines the treachery of the conspirators simply as a hired murder, a contract killing undertaken for a French purse. On discovery, however, one of them, the Earl of Cambridge, hints at an ulterior motive:

> For me, the gold of France did not seduce,
> Although I did admit it as a motive
> The sooner to effect what I intended.
> (II.ii.151–3)

In fact the three men arraigned here historically represented the cause of the deposed Richard II; the Earl of Cambridge's ulterior motive was that of re-establishing the legitimate dynasty toppled by the Lancastrian's usurpation. Ultimately they succeeded in forming the Yorkist power in the Wars of the Roses, in murdering Henry's son and in putting three kings on the English throne. The narrowing down of this complex constitutional problem to a simple focus on the question of political loyalty is a characteristic achievement of Henry's style of government and a familiar mechanism of ideological coercion in times of war. Political dissent becomes treachery: internal difference is forced to collapse under the moral and ideological pressures of international conflict.[11]

Kenneth Branagh placed particular emphasis on his decision to reinstate sections of the play-text omitted from Laurence Olivier's film version, and in particular the whole of Act II, scene ii:

> I decided on including some significant scenes that Olivier's film, for obvious reasons, had left out: in particular, the conspirators' scene where Henry stage-manages a public cashiering of the bosom friends who have been revealed as traitors. The violence and extremism of Henry's behaviour and its effect on a volatile war cabinet were elements that the Olivier version was not likely to spotlight.[12]

The general line of comparison here is that Olivier's film treatment was severely constrained by its wartime context of production: as a patriotic celebration of Britain's military strength and resolve, sponsored by the Ministry of Information, indissolubly linked both psychologically and strategically with the projected (and, of course, successful) Allied invasion of occupied France, the film was unlikely to place any emphasis on internal treachery, or to foreground qualities in Henry's character and behaviour that might be read as unpleasantly 'violent' or 'extreme'.

Both film versions establish this scene by adapting the device of Shakespeare's Chorus. In the Olivier version, a painting of the white cliffs of Southampton/Dover frames an unmistakably theatrical set, the prow of a stage ship where Henry and his nobles receive the sacrament before embarking. The overtly theatrical quality of the scene relates it closely to the reconstructed Elizabethan stage on which all the earlier scenes have been played. In the Branagh version Derek Jacobi as Chorus appears on a cliff-top (white, of course) from which he delivers the prologue to Act II. The sequence of directions reads:[13]

> *The Chorus is standing on a grassy cliff edge, looking out to sea. He turns to look at the camera.*
> CHORUS
>> The French, advised by good intelligence
>> Of this most 'dreadful' preparation … .
> *He turns to look towards the cliff top and we cut closer to the traitors who have now appeared, passing through the frame as their names are mentioned.*
> CHORUS
> One, Richard Earl of Cambridge …
> *As he walks away along the cliff edge, wrapping his scarf around him against the cold sea air, beyond him we see the dramatic white cliffs of the English coastline.*

Once the dramatic action is resumed, the Chorus disappears (though in the original theatrical production he frequently remained on stage) and the 'traitor scene' is established firmly in a naturalistic 'hostelry' (p. 36). The action is also played naturalistically, with a consistent emphasis on individual emotion. The key issue here is personal rather than political; the key emphasis falls on the shocking treachery of Henry's friends, particularly his 'bed-fellow' the Earl of Cambridge. At one point Henry throws Cambridge over a table with an almost sexual intensity, violently enacting the pain of personal betrayal (s.d. p. 40, illustration

p. 41). The conspirators confess only their guilt: Cambridge's lines about an alternative motive are cut.

The main interest in the scene as presented here consists in a dramatisation of the psychological stresses and strains of such a critical situation, as experienced in Henry's character. The dominant device of close-up is used here, as throughout the film, to register the psychological costs of authority. Branagh's intention may have been to foreground the violence and extremism of Henry's behaviour: but the naturalistic medium ensures that the nature of the spectator's engagement with the action is one of individual identification. Branagh's use, in the quotation on p. 88, of theatrical metaphors – 'stage-manages', 'spotlight' – actually draws attention to the *anti-theatrical* medium of filmic naturalism, in which very little space is left for the spectator to reflect on the nature of the dramatic medium itself. No one could gather from this scene, any more than from Olivier's version of the same scene, that there is implicit in the dramatic text a subtext related to the critical question of legitimacy. Branagh has conspired with the character of Henry himself to obliterate the play's momentary exposure of a stress-point in the unity of the commonwealth. In this way the possibility of political dissent can be completely occluded, both within and through the text, since all political opposition is converted on this ideological terrain to civil treachery and personal betrayal.

The key difference between the two film versions seems to me to reside in their respective adaptations of Shakespeare's Chorus. I have argued elsewhere[14] that Olivier's adaptation of the Chorus, and his initial setting of the production-text within a reconstructed Elizabethan theatre, put into circulation some of the 'radical and subversive potentiality of Shakespeare's play ... to foreground the artificiality of its dramatic devices'. Branagh's adaptation of the Chorus is equally inventive and in many ways effective. The device of beginning with the Chorus in an empty film studio, and opening set doors on to the dramatic action, is an ingenious updating of Olivier's mock Globe theatre. Though the Chorus is sometimes shown to be involved in the action (e.g. at the siege of Harfleur), he more characteristically appears as an alienation effect, emerging surprisingly from behind a tree after the execution of Bardolph, or appearing to block out the final scene of diplomatic reconciliation in the French court, where he delivers that sharply undercutting prophecy which calls into question Henry's political achievement. But the radical departure from Olivier's use of this device rests in the fact that although the Chorus becomes involved in the action, the action never strays on to the territory of the Chorus. At one point in the original Royal Shakespeare Company stage production, Henry and the Chorus, in a brilliant *coup de theâtre*, almost bumped into one another, miming a surprised double-take of near-recognition: with a shock of delight we saw the fictional world of the dramatic action suddenly enter the fictionalising activity of the Chorus. But in the film the naturalism of the action itself is never compromised in this way, despite the self-reflexive interventions of the intrusive choric witness.

It is abundantly clear, despite its radical features, in what relation Olivier's film stood to the nationalistic ideology of its time. But where does the Branagh film stand in relation to contemporary patriotic and nationalist ideologies? The original (1984) stage production, directed by Adrian Noble, and in which Branagh played the king, became known as the 'post-Falklands' *Henry V*. That suggests, of course, a prevailing mood of revulsion against war, against imperialistic shows of strength, against militaristic patriotism. The film can easily be read in line with this view: it was 'made for a generation with the Indo-China war and the Falklands behind it and is wary of calls to arms', according to Philip French.[15] Branagh has 'stripped the veneer of jingoism from the play and shown war in its true horror';[16] the film 'emphasises the horror and futility of battle'.[17]

But the term 'post-Falklands' may not be quite as simple as that. 'Post' (as in 'post-modernism') does not always translate easily as 'anti' or 'counter': and it could well be that along with the obvious political advantages accruing to the power victorious in a military conflict, the Falklands war bequeathed to British culture a decidedly unambiguous interest in war, not entirely unconnected with the characteristic emotions of patriotism. Certainly many of the post-Falklands cultural productions, such as Charles Wood's play *Tumbledown*,[18] betray a fascination with the experience of combat, with soldierly camaraderie, with the anguish of extreme suffering and with the psychological stresses of military leadership. Branagh's approach to the character of *Henry V*[19] was certainly to some degree founded on exactly such a fascination with the moral and emotional complexities made available in the theatre of war. His notorious consultation of Prince Charles,[20] by way of research into the isolation of office and the loneliness of command, indicates a readiness to refer directly and to attend sympathetically to the contemporary experience of monarchical power. In the stage production he played the character of Henry so as to disclose those emotional complexities, to reveal weakness as well as strength, self-suppression as well as self-aggrandisement, personal loss as well as national victory. In that production the Brechtian device of the Chorus was able to offer a counterpoise to this open though ambivalent admiration for the heroic individual. In the relatively naturalistic medium of the film, and, of course, under Branagh's own direction, there is no such system of checks and balances to subvert the invitation to empathic identification with the psychology of power.

Again, if we compare the very different social roles of Olivier and Branagh, we would expect very different perspectives of the play to emerge. The one was almost a natural product of the English *ancien régime*, his manly shoulders practically designed for the touch of the regal sword; the other aggressively constructs his own social persona as the tough and ambitious boy from working class Belfast, determined to make it in the competitive market place of the British theatre, as impatient with traditional institutions and fossilised establishments as the young shock-troops of the Thatcherite Stock Exchange. Now it is quite evident that

Branagh's studious and systematic campaign of self-publicity, a strategy he obviously considers necessary to the fulfilment of his artistic ambitions, engages with the naturalistic medium of the film to provoke a structural parallelism between actor and hero.[21] This theme runs through all the reviews of the film. In deciding to make it, Branagh 'took on much the same odds as Henry did at Agincourt';[22] he 'has marshalled his forces as well as Henry led his army.'[23] 'Clearly he has some sort of affinity with the part of King Henry, but it doesn't seem an actorly affinity. Branagh too talks like a winner, and *Henry V* offers him better than any other play in the repertoire what might be called a yuppy dynamic, a mythology of success and self-definition rather than struggle.'[24]

A structural parallel is also perceived between the 'band of brothers' with whose help Henry achieves such extraordinary success, and the team of actors assembled by Branagh to make the film. Here in the reviews we encounter a series of metaphors which oddly and unselfconsciously link theatrical and militaristic vocabularies. 'Before shooting started, Branagh, like Henry, addressed his troops, his happy few, saying he wanted to make it a "company picture".'[25] 'There is already something of the spirit of Henry's happy few in the cast and crew behind the camera ... every member of this film unit would go to the wall for Kenneth Branagh.'[26] 'The actors ... beamed like the happy few, ready to cry God for Kenneth.'[27]

Even odder is a tendency, quite in the spirit of that great tradition of public school patriotism which identified hand grenades with cricket balls, to express the relationship between theatre and heroic combat in metaphors of sport. Branagh himself dubbed his team 'the English all-stars', and several critics quipped along the same hearty and sporting lines: 'Branagh has fielded the first XV.'[28] 'This is how Englishmen play their football, so it seems a perfectly natural style in which to wage their wars.'[29] 'The English take Harfleur with the help of one horse and the first XI.'[30] Alexander Walker described Branagh as resembling 'a rugby forward who collects a bloody nose on the battlefield'.[31] We don't have to search for long among these testaments of reception to observe the repressed spirit of patriotic emotion returning in these attenuated forms.

Lastly there is the crucial relationship between this film as a cultural product, and the kind of cultural pattern being forged by Branagh in his entrepreneurial interventions into the theatrical economy. He stands for a reaction against the established national institutions of theatre, such as the Royal Shakespeare Company, and for the development of a privatised theatrical economy, with organisations like his own Renaissance Theatre Company supported by private and corporate sponsorship. Those who also approve of such developments are filled with passions of admiration when they contemplate Branagh's audacity, energy, ambition, nerve, determination, etc., etc., right through the whole vocabulary of self-help and entrepreneurial capitalism. 'Branagh's blitzkrieg left the profession breathless at his nerve, his energy and his disregard for the obstacles.'[32] 'The cream of our classical talent and an army of extras, horses and stunt-men ... was in itself a saga of nail-biting crises surmounted by his calm certainty of what he wants to do, and unshakeable confidence in being able to do it.'[33] Emma Thompson, who is married to Branagh and who plays Katherine in the film, embraces the same free-market vocabulary of risk and initiative, linked with the heroic language of war: 'These are the warrior years. These are the times to take risks and do the big things we might not have the courage and energy for later on.'[34] Some critics offered a clear-sighted analysis, whether prompted by enthusiasm or reservation. Richard Corliss in *The Times* called Branagh 'an icon of Thatcherite initiative', and Adam Mars-Jones in *The Independent* proposed an exact model for the cultural dialectics involved: 'The real chemistry is not between actor and part, but between the idea of the star as entrepreneur and the idea of the king as a self-made man.'[35] Clearly the myth enacted in this film is capable of signifying at this level, perhaps even more readily than at the level of national culture and politics.

In general the emotions of patriotism and the politics of nationalism always involve, in any given historical situation, attachment to a particular section, group, class, 'team' or army which can be seen as bearing or leading the national destiny. At the same time in every historical situation there is a larger, more pluralistic and multiple, more complex and contradictory national collective which any sectarian nationalist ideology must ignore, deny or suppress. The most natural context for this operation to be successfully conducted is that of war: and we have seen in the dramatisation of Henry V's policy how it can be done. We also know from our own experience of the Falklands war that it is possible for a government voted into power by 40 per cent of the population, and an army voted into power by nobody, to become self-appointed bearers of the entire nation's moral consciousness.

Raphael Samuel suggests that in contemporary Britain patriotic and nationalist feeling has sought and found a new home in the concept of the individual.[36]

> Orwell wrote in 1940 that the 'privateness' of English life was one of the secrets of its strength ... his account anticipates some major themes in post-war British life, in particular the break-up, or erosion, of corporate loyalties, and the increasingly home-centred character of British social life. Patriotism, on the face of it, is one of the victims of those developments. Yet it may be that, denied expression in the public sphere, it is finding subliminal support in the semiotics of everyday life.
>
> ... Individualism also has more solid material supports. The spread of home ownership, the sale of council houses, and the inflation of house prices has renewed the importance of family wealth and given a whole new terrain to Lockean notions of private property. The revival of small businesses – a feature of British as of other post-industrial societies – is multiplying the number of home-based or family-run concerns, while the dispersal of employment shows signs of reunifying work and home. Ideologically, public spirit is much less highly regarded than it was in the 1930s and 1940s. On both Left and Right of the political spectrum, self-expression is treated as the highest good, individual rights as

sacrosanct, and the enlargement of personal freedom – or its protection – the ideal object of policy. Government, for its part, has
built a whole platform out of freedom of choice, making, or
attempting to make, health, insurance, pensions, and schooling
matters of individual responsibility, and turning non-intervention
into the highest of statesmanly tasks. As Margaret Thatcher put it
in one of her best-remembered maxims: 'There is no society, only
men and women and families.'

Branagh's film version of *Henry V* is very clearly a product of this
new age of individualism. It is in this respect that it differs so
sharply from the play-text of the 1590s and the Olivier film of the
1940s. Denied a home in nationalist politics, the emotional
resources of patriotism gravitate inexorably towards their true
heartland in the individualism of the entrepreneur, whose conquest of new economic and artistic worlds continually endorses
the cultural and ideological power of the old.

     Kenneth Branagh did not, however, become constituted as
such an individual subject, this 'icon of Thatcherite initiative',
without a complex process of cultural negotiation. The film also
has another history through which can be traced the possibilities
of its being read otherwise. Branagh is himself a product of working-class Protestant Belfast, as well as a fellow-countryman of
William Shakespeare, heir to the mantle of Lord Olivier and a
loyal subject of Prince Charles's mother. The question posed by
Shakespeare's Captain Macmorris – 'what ish my nation?' –
would at certain stages of his life, if now no longer, have been
capable of provoking in him an existential anxiety parallel to that
dramatic expression of confused and exasperated anger. When in
1970 his family, horrified by the growth of political violence in the
province, moved permanently to England (where his father had
already been working for some years) Branagh felt, according to
the testimony of his 'autobiography', 'like a stranger ... in a very
strange land'.[37] This initial condition of alienation was resolved
only by the assumption of 'dual nationality' in a divided self:
'After a year or so I'd managed to become English at school

and Irish at home' (p. 23). He lived, he acknowledges, a 'double life' (p. 24), perpetually conscious of a deep cultural difference masked by apparent assimilation and ethnic homogeneity.

Branagh's formative childhood experience was thus enacted on a highly significant marginal space of 'British' culture, close to another of those territorial borders on which the contradictions of a nationalist ideology become acutely visible. Born a British citizen, within the borders of the 'United' Kingdom, Branagh inherited a particular Irish sub-culture, that of a large working-class extended family on the edge of the Belfast docks. He was also heir, however, to the questionable advantages of that 'British' culture of self-improvement and meritocratic social mobility which took him eventually to RADA, the RSC and Kensington Palace. These social contradictions of divided culture and frag-mented nationality can be read immediately from the brash, ambitious, self-mocking, self-important, painfully unstable dis-course of Branagh's premature 'autobiography', a project in itself designed to consolidate a coherent social identity out of a fissured and contradictory social experience. They can also be read from the film which, despite its totalising attempt to relocate the prob-lems of national identity and international conflict within the charismatic individual, occasionally uncovers and discloses sur-prising depths of cultural anxiety.

This anxiety can be traced in a symptomatic moment of textual 'excess', a point where the filmic narrative discloses an ideological 'stress-point' by delivering an emotional effect which remains unexplained by the contingent dramatic circumstances. As the miraculous victory of Agincourt becomes apparent, Cap-tain Fluellen (played by Ian Holm) reminds Henry of the heroic deeds of his ancestor Edward, 'the Black Prince of Wales'. Fluellen offers a Celtic re-reading of Anglo-Norman history, celebrating the heroic deeds of Welsh men-at-arms at Crecy, and appropriat-ing Edward himself as an honorary Welshman. Branagh's screen-play interprets this exchange as follows:[38]

FLUELLEN
… I do believe your Majesty takes no scorn to wear the leek upon
Saint Davy's day.
*The power of the Welshman's simple feeling is too much for the king
who speaks the following through tears which he cannot prevent. He
is near collapse.*
HENRY V
I wear it for a memorable honour;
For I am Welsh, you know, good countryman.
The King breaks down, and the two men hug each other.

Such cinematic surges of emotional intensity are, of course, ambiguous in their effects and can be read in many ways. Here there are readily available psychological explanations: this is the bitter price of heroism and military success; the post-orgasmic melancholy of the victor, satiated on violence or the human cost of successful rule. Branagh's Henry also sheds tears at the hanging of Bardolph, the screenplay emphasising the 'enormous cost' to the King of this necessary exercise of impartial justice (pp. 71–4). More generally, the film's capacity to reduce its participants and observers to tears is frequently cited as a measure of its authenticity: After the shooting of Agincourt, Branagh 'went home exhausted and somehow defeated, and for no good reason burst into tears'[39] and Prince Charles is reputed to have been similarly 'reduced to tears' at a special preview.[40] The demonstrative parading of open grief may at first sight appear subversive of the values of tough masculinity, the rigid suppression of emotion required for the serious business of warfare. But it should be clear from the sodden royal handkerchief with which we began, that these tears are closer to those rituals of mourning (such as the militaristic memorial service of 'Remembrance Day') which represent rather a liturgical collusion with the ideology of patriotic war, than an emotional interrogation of its values.

The moment in the film of extreme emotional exchange between Fluellen and Henry is quite different from these examples. Neither the film-text nor the screenplay can adequately

explain its intensity and its excessive superabundance of significance. And that leaking out of embarrassingly public grief seems
to me to locate a fault-line in the film's hegemony: for the sudden
burst of reciprocal grief is linked by the dialogue with questions
of national identity. As we observe the dramatisation of an English king and a Welsh soldier plangently embracing in a symbolic
ritual of national unity, we also catch a momentary glimpse of an
Irishman weeping over the historical devastations of British
imperialism. Can we not then read through the film's imagery of
post-Agincourt 'carnage and wreckage' (p. 113) the smoking ruins
of that battlefield that is Ulster? And can we not catch in those
verminous men and women 'pillaging the bodies of the dead' (p.
113) a fleeting glimpse of the young Kenneth Branagh, joining in
the looting of a bombed-out Belfast supermarket?[41]

One of the most interesting details of Branagh's *Henry V* does
not appear in the film (and is not therefore in the published
screenplay, which is a record of the final edited version, not the
screenplay from which the film is developed). When shooting the
scene where the Chorus strides the white cliffs of Southamp-
ton/Dover (filmed in fact at Beachy Head exactly midway
between the two), Branagh tried to use the same location for
another sequence:[42]

> We tried unsuccessfully to get another shot which I had felt at one
> stage could open the movie – a pan across the French coastline
> eventually taking in the white cliffs of England and ending on the
> contemplative face of yours truly. The whole thing was accompa-
> nied by the 'hollow crown' soliloquy from *Richard II*, which
> seemed to express something of the message of our *Henry V*. The
> shot did not work, and I decided to drop the Richard anyway. It
> simply didn't belong.

Who, in that strangely elliptical and impersonal phrase, is 'yours
truly'? The actor or the role? English Harry or Irish Ken? The
doubling of identities is paralleled by a corresponding spatial
ambivalence: that camera-pan simultaneously offers a description of the point-of-view of King Henry, firmly established on his

own territory, contemplatively surveying the enemy coast and delivers an external view of the 'English' coast as it would be seen by an enemy, an invader – or an immigrant. Prompted by the echoing words of Richard II, a king ousted from his own territory by the usurper whose heir now literally occupies its commanding heights, and by the semiotic value latent in Branagh's 'dual identity', the spectator presented with this filmic moment would have had ample opportunity to appreciate the position of an internal émigré about to establish his own territorial rights by violently overthrowing another's.

What would this sequence, if included in the film, have signified? What are the underlying reasons for its exclusion? The speech in question from *Richard II* (Act III, scene ii, 144–77) is a penetrating interrogation of the realities of power. The state is about to fall into the hands of Bolingbroke, Henry V's father, and Richard's imagination is released to a vivid realisation of the difference between effective power and mere legitimacy. Richard has no property in the realm to bequeath to his heirs, only the experience of royal tragedy – 'sad stories of the deaths of kings'. The imagery of hollowness runs throughout the speech, taking in the hollow grave, the hollow crown and the 'wall of flesh' encircling the mortal life, which seems impregnable as a castle yet contains only a vulnerable, isolated life. If the king's body is mortal, then sovereignty is a mere pageant, a stage performance, and the real sovereign of the royal court is death, the 'antic' who parodies and mocks all seriousness. The awareness of royal tragedy expressed here is nothing less than the Divine Right of Kings inverted, hollowed out to disclose the true nature of power.[43]

In the projected additional scene of Branagh's film, Richard's challenging interrogation is placed exactly on the sharp white line of a territorial border. Located there, the insistent questioning of the speech goes beyond an expression of melancholy resignation at the emptiness of power (the kind of thing calculated to set Prince Charles clutching for the royal nose-rag), to an earnest

meditation on the nature of the peripheral delineations by which
such spaces of hollowness are bound and contained. If we read
that border as simultaneously the south coast of England, and the
border between Ulster and Eire, we can grasp simultaneously the
paradox of definition and arbitrariness, of clear geographical
division and constructed geopolitical disposition, which belongs
to all territorial borders, especially those between an imperialist
and a colonised nation. Travelling back to that mythical spot of
origins, which is simultaneously a possible point of exit (Beachy
Head is a favourite haunt of suicides), some of the fundamental
questions of British national identity can at last be posed. Does a
geographical boundary such as the English Channel prescribe
mutual hostility and reciprocal violence between the neighbouring nations?

> the contending kingdoms
> Of France and England, whose very shores look pale
> With envy of each other's happiness,
> May cease their hatred
>
> (*Henry V*, V.ii.377–9)

The inclusion of that speech from *Richard II*, significantly poised
on the edge of England, could have hollowed out an illuminating
space between actor and character: a disclosure which could have
expressed these cultural contradictions even more eloquently, if
the film had found a means of including Shakespeare's reference
to Essex, returning from Ireland, 'bringing Rebellion broached on
his sword'.

Meanwhile, as the film cameras whirred on a summit of
Beachy Head, constructing a sequence destined to become a hollow absence of the film-text, far below and out to sea, other kinds
of machinery were simultaneously hollowing out a link between
'the contending kingdoms'. The 'Chunnel', when completed, will
rob the white cliffs of much of their centuries-old symbolism. For
once Britain is physically part of Europe, the ideological stress on
ancient national mythologies will be enormously intensified. The
interesting combination, on the part of Britain's Tory govern-

ment, of pro-European commitment and chauvinistic resistance to European union, testifies to the problems facing British national ideology. The government's insistence on the private funding of what is self-evidently a public construction project (leading to an endless series of financial crises), and the anxieties frequently expressed about what kinds of contamination may enter the realm once a major transport artery is plugged deep into its vitals (those who applaud the demolition of the Berlin Wall tend, when contemplating the Chunnel, towards extravagant fantasies of invasion by terrorists and rabid animals), indicate deep ideological ambivalences towards the destruction of a 'natural' boundary. Some residual reverence for the acculturated sanctity of the south coast even underlies reasonable conservationist anxieties about the fate of the white cliffs themselves; focusing as they do in particular on a spot some distance from the site of the tunnel itself, but legitimated by its very name as a space of that England (one of which, according to the words of another popular wartime song, there will always be), and which various parties for different reasons would wish to be conserved: Shakespeare Cliff, near Dover.

CHAPTER FIVE

Heritage (1992)

৵

WHAT IS 'HERITAGE'? It is not the past, but that which survives from the past, and is 'inherited' in the present. It is not history, but the traces of a vanished existence, the footprint that
marks the passing of an earlier age. But heritage is a very selective
processing of history, a structured abstraction from the past. As
individuals we can inherit desirable goods such as money and
houses; we can also inherit syphilis and sickle-cell anaemia. When
undesirable realities, such as poor housing and disease, survive
from the past into the social present, no one refers to these as part
of 'our' heritage. So a more precise definition of heritage, still
within the metaphor of personal inheritance, would be those
things which we ought to be pleased to have left to us. At this
point historical intention or accident becomes moral obligation:
since we ought, having inherited these things, also to be prepared
to look after and 'conserve' them.

This of course raises the crucial question of ownership. A
concept like 'the national heritage' may include things in public
ownership, but may well consist much more substantially of
things owned (and inherited) by private individuals and families.
One of the first strategies of the 'heritage' movement, enacted
through the National Trust, was the Country House Act of 1937,
by means of which the costs of maintaining such houses could
become the responsibility of the state, in return for limited rights

of public access, while the owners could continue to occupy the house and bequeath it to their heirs. Public access to the 'national heritage' often consists not in ownership but visiting rights. Millions of people do however exercise those rights: statistics suggest that more people visit museums and country houses than patronise theatres, dance and opera houses.[1]

'Heritage' remains curiously undefined at the level of government policy and legislative framework, despite two Acts of Parliament centred on the concept (the National Heritage Acts, 1980 and 1983, which established respectively the National Heritage Memorial Fund and English Heritage). In their first annual report, the trustees of the National Heritage Memorial Fund declared that they 'could no more define heritage than ... beauty or art'. At the theoretical level the term is therefore open, both for arbitrary definition and for contestation.[2] One of the most significant shifts, enabled by this absence of theoretical focus, in the practical application of the term over recent years has been an adjustment in the relationship between heritage and ownership. There is now, for example, a recognition of the industrial past (which may, of course, be of relatively recent origin) as subject to considerably more rapid processes of decay and disappearance than the Georgian country house, and therefore in equally urgent need (if worth preserving) of conservation. Industrial archaeology thus becomes as legitimate a conservationist cause as the excavation of Roman or medieval remains; and its results equally deserving of exhibition. At the same time, an application of modern social history to the concept of heritage produces a positive evaluation of the everyday domestic lives of millions over against the public lives of a few: so it becomes feasible to construct a 'heritage centre' or exhibition around, say, regional working class life in the early twentieth century. Alongside the national museums in London arise the Wigan Pier Heritage Centre, the Beamish Open Air Museum, and countless similar commemorative displays and enactments of 'ordinary living' in the past. Patrick Wright has written of the post-war expansion which has widened out the repertoire of the National Heritage, establishing the ordinary street alongside the mansion and the industrial relic alongside the great artistic masterpiece. In this way conflicting cultures may well come to be combined in a bland celebration of mere diversity, but one should never forget that this expansion has often followed an active *claiming* of national significance in the name of previously excluded cultures and interests.[3]

Museums too have changed their emphasis from the acquisition, curation and exhibition of objects to an investment in 'hands-on' activities, simulated displays, audio-visual performances. Recently the most popular of the London museums was the Museum of the Moving Image which commemorated the far from remote history of cinema and broadcasting in a virtual reality of high-tech, user-friendly client participation.

Though mostly state-subsidised, in one way or another, these new 'heritage' enterprises are market-led, commercial operations. Their commercial context is the leisure and services industry; their direct market, tourism. They often represent a form of damage-containment recuperation when, for example, industrial plants and communities, rendered obsolete by the rapidity of economic change, are reconstructed as industrial museums. In the key works of cultural analysis addressed to these developments,[4] they are perceived as evidence of a process of economic and cultural decline: a systematic substitution of replica for reality, simulation for experience, enactment for lived history.

~❧

The village of Avebury in Wiltshire is known as the site of a ring of megalithic stones. Like Stonehenge, these objects are genuine survivors, veterans of the long struggle against time. They derive therefore (unlike, for example, the many traces of Roman occupation) from a remote historical past about which very little is known. They are for this reason mysterious in a literal sense: nobody knows the reason or purpose of their erection. Far less well known than Stonehenge, they are not particularly firmly positioned on a tourist itinerary, not normally reached via any ritual passage to a site heavily sacralised by the liturgies of the heritage industry. Most people see them, as I first did, by accident: probably driving along a back road to avoid traffic congestion.

The stones are strange because they are not normal occupants of a modern agricultural field; though this need have no connection with antiquity, applying equally to the famous concrete cows of Milton Keynes. They are strange because they are inexplicable, and therefore present no impediment to the free imagination of the observer. They are sources of historical knowledge only in a very limited sense, because there is so little information to contextualise them into a framework of reasonable hypothesis. We encounter them as alien, as strangers from another world: we do not understand their language, their customs, their culture. They are, to use a term of Walter Benjamin's, adapted and applied to the analysis of heritage by Donald Horne, 'auratic':[5] capable of stimulating, or of being constituted within, a response of mysterious emotional affectivity. This 'aura' (which we will meet again later in the form of a curious phenomenon known as the 'tingle factor') is clearly dependent on some frame of cultural competence. It does not consist of some mysterious potency lurking within the stones, but rather of a kind of dislocation in normal habits of perception, the shock of coming up against historical difference. Here the past can be encountered by chance as an alien power which has come and gone, leaving behind these strange, inscrutable messengers holding an unintelligible secret. They impress without communicating; they provoke curiosity without supplying knowledge; they stimulate interest without satisfying understanding.[6]

W. Benyon, Tory MP for Buckingham, during the second reading of the National Heritage Bill (1980), concisely defined heritage as 'that which moulders'. This is, of course, exactly what time does to buildings and other cultural objects; it rots them.

Historicity is defined as much by a propensity to decay as by a persistence in surviving. Buildings made to last have a history different from buildings designed to obsolesce. The dwellings of Saxon farmers, and some of the tower-blocks of 1960s urban development, fell down, while the castles of the Anglo-Norman aristocracy survived, for fairly substantial historical reasons. If the history of a Tudor manor house (or of a Stratford-upon-Avon town-house) is a history of dilapidation, then that is its history, the story it has to tell us about relations between past and present. If no one goes to look at it, if it is effectively non-existent, then that absence from public consciousness is also a historical reality. Robert Hewison distinguishes between 'preservation' and 'conservation':

> Preservation means the maintenance of an object or building, or such of it as remains, in a condition defined by its historic context, and in such a form that it can be studied with a view to revealing its original meaning. Conservation, on the other hand, creates a new context and a new use.[7]

Close to the Avebury stones is Avebury Manor, a Tudor dwelling-house that had fallen into disuse and decay: unoccupied, dilapidated, crumbling. In 1989 a London builder and small businessman, Ken King, bought Avebury Manor with a determination to reverse the inexorable judgement of time. For Ken (who presents himself as an Arthur Dailey figure and describes himself as a 'Jack-the-lad-entrepreneur') the crumbling building no longer represented a real history. To look at an empty, decaying ruin gives the observer no sense at all of what such a house would have been in its earlier centuries of existence – a busy, populous centre of social and administrative life on an estate, a centre of social, cultural, commercial and productive activity. Ken's scheme was to restore the Manor to its original character by converting it into a kind of Elizabethan theme park. The circulation of people and traffic which would have made the Manor a lively and populous place can be replaced by the circulation of tourists and

school parties. The vanished inhabitants of the house can be simulated by attendants and guides in period costume. The house
itself could be virtually rebuilt (by, for example, temporarily
removing the roof in order to restructure the walls) to restore it
to its former fortunes. An 'Elizabethan experience' would become
available in a 'living museum'. In a TV programme devoted to this
instance of heritage recuperation, comments were sought from a
cross-section of local inhabitants. The broadcaster Ludovic
Kennedy, who lives nearby as a weekend villager, found it difficult
to walk his bearded collie in peace among the bulldozers and felt
that the Manor should be left as it was for the enjoyment of people like himself. A local lady shrilly objected to the despoliation of
'her' heritage and to the undesirable types of people who would
be drawn into the area. An elderly man from a local council estate
thought it a very good scheme which might bring employment to
the area: after all, the house wasn't doing anyone any good as it
was.

❧

The megalithic stones and the Tudor manor house of Avebury
represent the parameters within which the heritage industry
transacts its commercial and ideological business: preservation
and conservation, the monument and the theme park, the reality
and the replica, the surviving historical trace and the re-enact-
ment of history as 'living museum'. Precisely the same binary
opposition constituted one of the strange cultural and political
relationships formed as a consequence of the emergence, into
daylight and public consciousness, of the foundations of the Rose
Theatre, excavated by Museum of London archaeologists early in
1989: the relationship between the International Globe Trust's
replica Elizabethan theatre, under construction on Bankside, and
the 'real foundations' on which such reconstructions must super-
structurally rest. Sam Wanamaker's project of 'rebuilding' the
Globe Theatre was challenged and compromised in interesting

ways through the turning up, by an archaeologist's trowel, of an old competitor, the Rose.

The London Globe reconstruction project can claim over any rival a unique and unchallengeable advantage: its replica of 'Shakespeare's theatre' stands near to the site of the original theatre (now also rediscovered and partially excavated). The relationship between project and place, traced in John Drakakis's essay 'Shakespeare and the Roadsweepers',[7] involves more than history. Initially the Globe project was formulated both as a 'popular theatre' and as a community enterprise; the revival of a democratic drama and the renewal of a local culture; the resurrection of the Globe and the restoration of cultural and economic vitality to a depressed urban locality. Once the Globe Trust had in 1986 emerged victorious from its legal battle over use of the land with Southwark Council, there appeared a marked shift in its public position, from attachment to an unsympathetic local authority and an unsupportive local community, to dependence on local business, the Royal family and the Tory government. Aspirations to represent the revival of popular theatre and the rehabilitation of an economically derelict area became subordinated to the commercial and touristic components of the enterprise.[8]

It thus became clear that for the Globe project, the support of a 'local community' was, as John Drakakis observed, 'a conveniently variable factor in the equation'[9]. The demographic and social justifications of the Globe's location virtually dispensed with the relationship between project and site then resolved themselves into an apparently simpler question of historical continuity. The fact that the theatre had been destroyed three centuries previously was not considered an insurmountable objection to the project of its relocation: if a historical monument is no longer there to be seen, all you have to do is build a replica on the original site and you recapture not only the appearance but the 'spirit' of the original. This was certainly Sam Wanamaker's view:

> To visit a place or site for its historical associations is to acquire an

experience. To visit the ruins of an important historical centre is to acquire an experience. To visit a replica or reconstruction is not quite the same, yet such places can acquire the patina of the original ... a reconstructed Globe ... will absorb the spirit of the original theatre. People who come to it – whether in superficial curiosity, reverential love or deep appreciation – will experience something of the past[10].

The term 'patina' denotes an interesting semantic process. Initially, the encrusted corruption of oxidisation on the surface of bronze, it became descriptive first of the real texture of age on any other material surface, and then of the appearance of such a texture as it can be simulated when works are art are 'antiqued'. Waldemar Januszczak described this transition:[11]

> The texture of poverty used to be called 'patina'. It is the appearance of old age, a kind of spurious spirituality endowed upon the art work by the passage of time.

When 'patina' becomes something to add to a new object to make it look old, it is

> that warm, worn, safe, familiar feeling worshipped by immature societies shell-shocked from progress. Post-modern collectors buy new art covered in patina for the same reason as post-modern architects build Neo-Georgian buildings, to gain a respite from the decision-making processes of the present. They are literally buying second-hand time.

By a mysterious osmotic process the new Globe will acquire, according to Wanamaker, from the site of the old, an authentic veneer of antiquity. A moment's observation of the site in question would produce a certain scepticism on this score. It is, however, a characteristic strategy of 'heritage' to affirm the contiguity of the present and past. An old world can be 'entered' simply by stepping off the present on to a plane of imaginative reality continuous with the past. In one of the 'Shakespeare in Perspective' broadcasts introductory to the BBC Shakespeare series, George Melly stood in the middle of Shrewsbury and remarked: 'the city traffic may roar past outside ... but here for a moment the real estate agent from Dallas, the insurance clerk from south-east London may enjoy an hour or two in a simpler, more gay world.' Patrick Wright comments:

> A national heritage site must be sufficiently of this world to be accessible by car or camera, but it must also encourage access to that other 'simpler' world when the tourist or viewer finally gets there ... this publicly instituted transformation between prosaic reality and the imagination of a deep past is central to the operation of the national heritage ... these sites exist only to provide that momentary experience of utopian gratification in which the grey torpor of everyday life in contemporary Britain lifts and the simpler, more radiant measures of Albion declare themselves again.[12]

The relationship between this contemporary experience of 'transformation' and the past itself can be complex. It may involve the presence of ancient buildings, monuments and objects though these may not necessarily occupy their original places. The Beamish Open Air Museum near Newcastle contains a railway station, miners' cottages, a Co-operative store, colliery workings – all of which have been transported from somewhere else and rebuilt on a single site. Or it may, as in the case of the Globe, involve total replication, using conjecturally 'authentic' materials from the present but nothing that survives from the past. This contradictory balance of considerations could obviously be thrown into serious disequilibrium by the emergence, literally next door to the Globe's 'heritage' site, of a material heritage consisting of actual relics from the past, surviving, physical objects such as the foundations of the Rose theatre.

~

The site of the Rose theatre, built around 1587, clearly marked on nineteenth century Ordnance Survey maps of the area, was built over in 1957 by Southbridge House. This building, ironically an

element in the 'urban renewal' of Bankside (inaugurated by the
Festival of Britain[13] in 1951, which in turn was intended to herald
a 'Second Elizabethan Age') was constructed by driving foundation posts right through the buried site of the theatre. Thirty
years later it had become, according to the standards of modern
property developers and the current value of land, 'obsolete'.
Planning permission was granted by Southwark Council to the
Heron Group for the building of an office block, subject to the
condition that archaeologists must be allowed access to excavate
any remains. Under a voluntary code of practice drawn up in
1986 by the British Archaeological Trust and the Developers Liai-
son Group, developers are obliged to pay for archaeological work
designed to excavate any significant sites to be built on, in
exchange for the archaeologists' agreement not to hold up development work unnecessarily, not to campaign publicly against the
interests of the developer and so on. The Heron Group had
offered the Museum of London eight weeks for site evaluation,
and a further unspecified period to be negotiated, when it sold
the site to developers Imry Merchant. New plans appeared for a
bigger office block, and for all required archaeological work only
the eight weeks already offered for site evaluation alone.

In the event, the developer's optimistic timetable was held up
by the discovery of the Rose foundations and by the public campaign that followed. The campaign itself was part local community action (it was led by Southwark and Bermondsey MP Simon
Hughes), part agitation of the conservation lobby, part histrionic
militancy on the part of leading members of the theatrical and
entertainment profession and part intelligible (indeed, quite
laudable) routine resistance to absolutely anything a London
property developer wishes to undertake. The principal objective
of the campaign in the first instance was to persuade the Department of the Environment to 'schedule' the remains of the Rose so
that development would be prevented. To 'schedule' an ancient
monument is the equivalent of 'listing' a building: in each case,
the site acquires protection from potentially destructive develop-

ment. Environment Secretary Nicholas Ridley, true to form on such matters, declined to schedule the Rose. Bowing to media pressure and presenting themselves as conservationists, Imry Merchant agreed to redesign their office block so that the Rose remains would be preserved for further excavation and eventual display: their design became known as the 'office on stilts'. The 'Save the Rose' campaign insisted from the outset that the site should be left undeveloped, with the Rose preserved and present-ed for public display (this strategy was poetically termed the 'Blue Skies' option). The advice of English Heritage[14] a supposedly independent body which in this case appeared ably to represent the interests of government and developers, was that in view of the development timetable (which under the Voluntary Code should not be disturbed) the Rose site should be 'back-filled', to be excavated at a later date (i.e. when the office block was demol-ished). In the end it was the developer's option that was imple-mented. The Rose was submerged in concrete to be subsequently re-excavated, the office block redesigned to permit building at an elevation over the site and the drilling of its concrete piles around rather than through the foundations of the theatre.

The International Shakespeare Globe Centre (ISGC) partici-pated in the Save the Rose campaign. It took due cognisance of its significance in contradicting many suppositions about Elizabethan playhouses (when the Globe foundations were later excavated, the ISGC stopped their own building work to assimi-late any surprising archaeological discoveries into its design), incorporated much discussion of the Rose excavation into its own publicity and constructed an exhibition about the Rose in the Bear Gardens Museum. None the less there were severe politi-cal tensions between the two campaigns, ranging from the pre-dictable to the bizarre. Sam Wanamaker, with a great deal of his own fund-raising target still to achieve, obviously did not think the charitable economy could sustain two campaigns: 'If they [the Save the Rose campaign] start a public fund-raising drive it could be damaging to our campaign.' The fear of competition entailed a comparative evaluation of reality and replica: 'Of course I'm worried that they want to raise millions of pounds for the Rose. People can only look at the site for five minutes, and that's it.'[15]

The ISGC clearly regarded itself, rather than the Rose campaign, as the appropriate custodian of the foundations: the ISGC plan proposed incorporating a preserved Rose into its own Bear Gardens Museum. This somewhat high-handed assumption of natural stewardship even extended to the ISGC's blocking of a Rose Campaign plan to use, as their logo, the 'universal' image of Shakespeare! When in July 1989 Southwark Council's Planning Committee considered the various options proposed for the future of the Rose, beside the Rose Campaign Committee's persistent adherence to the 'Blue Skies' option (that the foundations should be preserved and exhibited without being built over) there was a letter from Sam Wanamaker on behalf of the ISGC, advocating acceptance of the property developer's plan (the 'office on stilts'):[16]

> The issue of the Rose has been protracted over several months and has caused some confusion and a serious deflection of effort from our own fund-raising and educational activities. With the additional revisions now proposed, we strongly urge your committee to act decisively to approve the Imry application so that we can move on to the many urgent issues regarding the future development of Bankside.

This position approximates closely to that of Ken King, Lord of Avebury Manor. By a peculiar reversal the replica Globe becomes the 'real thing', while the 'real foundations' of the Rose become a mere distraction. Sam Wanamaker's 'five minutes' is compatible with other equally dismissive definitions like Bernard Levin's 'a hole in the ground', Terry Dicks's 'a pile of bricks and rubble', Joan Bakewell's 'not even a building'.

The Globe and the Rose were constituted within this discourse into a series of classic binary oppositions: centre and margin, high and low priority, senior and junior partner, Shakespearean and not-really-Shakespearean, mature Shakespearean and early Shakespearean, even male and female. Frequently in both supportive and dismissive public comment, the Rose was implicitly gendered as conventionally female: a 'sleeping beauty', awoken and put to sleep again by technological enchantment; a fragile body, in need of chivalric protection; then a Juliet, dead in her tomb, buried by an 'impermeable membrane', a restored virginity in concrete. The developer's building work was imagined as a kind of rape, as Imry Merchant threatened to drive huge 8-foot-thick concrete piles through 'the very heart of the Rose'. Others stressed the pointlessness of a 'hole in the ground', a no-thing about which it seemed fatuous to conduct too much ado. The Globe in this discursive strategy was implicitly male, but could easily be transformed into an image of legitimate femininity, approved because properly occupied – the site of a 'Wooden O' into which so manly a character as Prince Philip was prepared to drive his ancient oaken post.[17]

It is initially tempting simply to invert this initial binary opposition, and to claim the Rose as 'real' and 'authentic' against the 'simulated reality' of the Globe. In some basic material sense this is obviously the case. The excavation of the Rose conferred on its remains the power of evidence, a capacity to controvert speculative assumptions about the nature of Elizabethan theatres. The Rose, with its shallow stage facing the wrong way, its sloping yard, its most un-Vitruvian 13-sided irregular polygonal structure, was able to inform scholarship, to challenge opinion and to change minds. 'The Rose', said C. Walter Hodges, 'has thrown all our established working premises and assumptions into disarray'.[18]

The Globe, of course, for all the ISGC's concern with accuracy in imitation and authenticity of detail, occupies quite a different order of 'reality'. To reconstruct a building using 'original' materials and 'authentic' construction techniques still gives you a modern building, however imitative of earlier models. Further, the design concept within which the Globe will be incorporated is

enthusiastically post-modern in its eclecticism, pastiche, quotations of antique styles: 'The Centre will be a collection of interconnected buildings, each separately expressed with its own
character. Although not copies of older buildings, they will use
clues such as original materials and proportions to *evoke memories of past techniques*' (my italics).[19]

-&-

But can we rest the argument on a basis as tenuous as a binary
opposition between 'reality' and the 'unreal'? The chalk pillars,
mortar, lath, plaster and hazlenut shells of the Rose excavation
provide a kind of scientific knowledge. They offer an alternative
configuration of data on which basis new speculation, like the
original building, can be founded. That scientific knowledge is,
by definition, a concern of specialists. The evidence could not
even be produced for observation except by the professional
expertise of archaeologists. Further archaeological analysis is then
needed for evaluation and explanation of the physical objects and
traces disclosed. Historical scholarship can then set to work on
the task of interpretation. All this is clear and uncontroversial.
But this is specialist history, not popular heritage; for the few, not
for the many. The information gathered from an archaeological
excavation takes on general meaning and value only when translated on to paper or computer screen, only when circulated and
mobilised in the service of a scientific or educational programme.
Archaeological sites are in themselves often unintelligible to a
non-specialist. The strikingly clear photographs of the Rose
foundations in outline were taken from the top of a tower block:
only distance and aerial perspective could contextualise the
remains so as to render them generally intelligible.

If what we are interested in is historical knowledge, initially
for the interpretation of specialists, then this has nothing to do
with the conservation and display of an archaeological excavation.[20] To gather the maximum of information from an archaeo-

logical site, it is necessary to destroy it: to remove every piece of evidence, in order the more effectively to analyse and test it. Only in this way can all the data be recovered. 'Rescue archaeology' is often thought of as the melodramatic snatching of some fragile remains from the path of the developer's bulldozer, rather like the chivalric untying of a heroine from under the advancing wheels of a train. But archaeological remains often need rescuing from an enemy even more powerful than the property developer. The physical nature of the object in this case actually made 'rescue archaeology' the most sensible option: the Rose was built of materials which decay quickly once exposed to the air, preserved in the first place only by burial and the dampness of the soil. Once exhumed and exposed, they begin to decay rapidly, requiring special covering and continual watering.

Does it make sense to conserve something primarily of interest to specialists, if those interests would best be served by 'rescue archaeology', the total excavation of the site? If a site is presented for a broader constituency who might wish or be persuaded to visit and observe, can it be left in a form meaningful to archaeologists, but indecipherable to anyone else? Doesn't the site require what is known as 'enhancement', or what Donald Horne has called 'exposition' – which at the level of minimal interference means little explanatory signs for the convenience of the visitor's orientation; but at the maximal level means the construction of something like Yorvik, the excavated site of a Viking settlement in York which has become the ultimate heritage train-ride. The Save the Rose campaign committee has commissioned a feasibility study for the representation of the Rose, once re-excavated, from Heritage Projects, the consultants who created Yorvik.

The Save the Rose campaign was, of course, conducted around an un-enhanced, un-exposed site. So as far as its members and supporters were concerned, the remains were self-evidently valuable and worth conserving in themselves. The campaign took a clearly principled stand on this, fighting continuously for conservation without development (which would have been possible only if the Secretary of State had agreed to schedule the Rose as an ancient monument, or if his negative ruling could have been successfully tested in law). In what did its value consist? The Rose was firmly identified as part of the national cultural heritage: in a message transmitted from Lord Olivier to the crowds on the site, 'part of one's heritage', which should not be 'swept under the concrete as if it had never existed'[21]. The famous actors and entertainers who drew the cameras and journalists to the site testified to a direct apprehension of heritage through physical proximity to the Rose site. 'I belong to the Rose,' said Ian McKellen, 'and that's where my voice should be heard'[22]. Judi Dench took off her shoes and stood barefoot on the stage, to get as close as possible to the recuperated past. There was much experiencing of the 'tingle factor', that communication of aura, that mysterious emotional vibration shared by many of the Rose's visitors. Philip Ormond of the theatre publicity firm Theatre Dispatch described the process exactly:

> – a patch of damp mud with some stones sticking out; an archaeologist's plan stapled to the hoarding, some cold minutes of cross-referencing the plan to the stones – an intellectual exercise, then suddenly, the site of the theatre clicked into place and I was standing where the best seats had been, looking down on the stage where Shakespeare had probably acted – a unique emotional experience.[23]

These appeals to a universal possession ('our heritage') are, of course, in actuality culturally specific. They derive from a particular cultural and ideological discourse, and when in operation they demonstrate the cultural competence of the speaker. This problem could be considered the inversion of the theme park version of heritage since it thrives on the meanness of the opportunities history affords; draws not on historical detail but imaginative liberty; flourishes not on the solidity of physical evidence but the active exercise of well-informed fantasy. The less there is in the way of physical evidence, the more authentic the sensibility

of the observer. Here is David Garrick on Shakespeare's birthplace – then, of course, a dilapidated building,[24] not the restored
original you see today:

> the humble shed, in which the immortal bard first drew that
> breath which gladdened all the isle, is still existing; and all who
> have a heart to feel, and a mind to admire the truth of nature and
> the splendour of genius, will rush thither to behold it, as a pilgrim
> would to the shrine of some loved saint; will deem it holy ground,
> and dwell with sweet though pensive rapture on the natal habita-
> tion of the poet.[25]

The humbler the 'shed', the more feeling the heart, the more
admiring the mind of the observer.

If, however, this invocation of a universal national culture is
simply an attempt on the part of a cultural élite to exercise and
demonstrate its influence then where does that leave the less cultivated witness – the contemporary observer, with a heart less
capable of conjuring from mud and rubble visions of the past
than any of Garrick's successors who filled the site of the Rose
with similarly apposite quotations? Once the actors have gone
back to work and the media circus has moved on, is not the subject of this natural consensus 'our national heritage' left rather
forlorn beside that 'hole in the ground', that 'pile of bricks and
rubble?'

◦

This leave us stranded interestingly between an empty hole and a
crowded theme park. The Save the Rose campaign clearly intends
that the secrets of that now once again far-off, secret, most invio-
late Rose should ultimately be revealed; not exclusively held for
specialists, but presented to the public as a national monument to
a common cultural heritage. But how can you show the true historical nature of that monument (an educational as well as commercial aspiration) to that public, except by 'exposition' and

'enhancement'? The argument, and the long-term strategy of the Rose campaign, point inexorably towards the theme park. The 'enhanced' site could, within the discourse of heritage, lay claim, like Yorvik, to greater authenticity by virtue of its resting on 'real foundations'. But so too, as we have seen, can a patently simulated reconstruction like the Globe. Since the process of enhancement is never less than a contemporary processing and appropriation of the past, subject to whatever ideological determinants may currently be in operation, are not such acts of recuperation and exposition always heritage rather than history? Once the Rose site has given up its being in the form of scientific knowledge, is there any essential difference, for public access and appreciation, between an enhanced Rose and a simulated Globe?

The claim to 'authenticity' in this particular context of heritage recuperation is inevitably spurious, since that which is authentic is likely to be incommunicable in heritage terms. If we are interested in promoting an unillusioned grasp of historical difference, then claims to historical originality and authenticity through the significance of place are a distraction, since they systematically blur the distinctions between past and present, history and heritage. This is a much more complex matter than simple fraud or imposture. When visitors to Stratford-upon-Avon enter a Tudor-looking building with the sign 'New Place' above the door, they are not necessarily being duped into believing that this structure is the original house occupied by Shakespeare and demolished in 1759. Appropriate and responsible 'exposition' informs them of the facts. But the historical distinction between the 'original' garden and the reconstructed building is systematically elided both by the physical homogeneity of reconstruction, and by the ideological deep structure of the tourist occasion itself which seeks the interface between present and past.[26]

A new Globe theatre on the South Bank of the Thames is, of course, a very different matter. Rising in extraordinary architectural isolation among the dereliction and tower-blocks, a reproduced Elizabethan theatre could represent a triumph of post-modern style, capable by its pastiche and quotation of calling attention simultaneously to present and past, a contradictory synthesis of modernity and the antique. The relationship between building and location would be one of shocking incongruity rather than any smooth absorption of a distinctive local patina. Stripped of all pretensions to authenticity, could not such a building offer the spectator a critical consciousness of cultural appropriation?

One of the most striking developments in heritage presentation, with the movement towards simulation by theme park and living museum, is the presence of live performers: not actors performing drama on a theatrical stage, but performers enacting a drama of everyday life in the theatre of a reconstructed history. The public representation of history has moved from the simple exhibition of objects, to static tableaux using dummies and waxwork effigies, through technologically mobilised active displays, to the enactment by living people of a historical drama. The intention may well have been to secure more 'lifelike' effects; the result, however, is performance, a new kind of theatre, and the essence of theatre is that it can simultaneously foster illusion and secure demystification. When a redundant South Wales miner plays the role of a miner in a pit-turned-colliery-theme-park, the distinction between the actor and his former role is as sharply significant as the continuity. In the more populist and democratic forms of heritage enterprise (as in new forms of community the-atre)[27] the relationship between past and present is problematised by the paradox of connection in discontinuity: there is an implicit estrangement-effect in the fact that the live performer is very much *not* the person impersonated.

The continued use in heritage attractions of dummies, together with more sophisticated forms of display technology, can thus be seen to possess virtues beyond those of cheapness and contractual simplicity. Possibly because a waxwork is in reality rather more like a dead than a living person, the effigy has a power of illusion beyond that of the live performer. A tourist centre in Stratford, previously 'The World of Shakespeare', and now renamed 'Heritage Theatre', contains a son-et-lumière display, using moving dummies, special effects and recorded sound, dramatising the 'Shakespeare's England' of Tillyard and Dover Wilson. The audience occupies a circular auditorium, darkened during the performance, and the spectacle takes place all around. The method is one of 'total theatre', with the spectator completely encircled by sound and vision; the performance culminates in an audio-visual simulation of a court masque. The vast and potent illusion of the Elizabethan World Picture is conveyed to the spectator through these theatrical resources far more completely than they could be communicated by any live performance. Ideological complicity, unresisted by an existing critical consciousness, can be guaranteed. The same spectators, confronted in Southwark Bridge Road by a figure clad in doublet and hose, would experience the pleasant, disorientating absurdity of all street theatre: but would be under no illusion as to the authenticity of the historical personage enacted.

᪇

One of the key theoretical difficulties in our current address to heritage is the foundation of all the major theoretical works in certain critical writings of the Frankfurt school, particularly Adorno and Horkheimer's *Dialectic of Enlightenment* (1944). From that seminal essay derives the very term 'the culture industry', within which conceptual framework the developments I have been discussing became available for analysis. Yet the structure of the Adorno-Horkheimer argument is framed by a set of extremely reactionary propositions: the ideological crisis created by the decline of traditional social institutions such as the family; the total reification of culture into a manipulative industry; the destruction of the autonomous individual, the degeneracy of the mass media, and the critical value of high culture.[28] It has proved difficult even for a socialist writer such as Patrick

White to acknowledge from within this totalising problematic any possibilities for resistance within the cultural activities of heritage. Yet clearly there are possibilities, visible even in some of the existing enterprises, for the production of an alternative heritage, a living theatre of the past capable of producing a grasp of historical difference. Robert Hewison's work, with its general distinction between the reality of the past and the attenuated imitations of the present, maps the space of popular culture as the unmitigated triumph of the culture industry.

Both writers frequently employ metaphors from theatre, invariably used to identify the artificial, the simulation, the illusion, the deception. Yet it is surely in performance that an unillusioned grasp of history might still be found, even within the heritage industry. And it is surely within popular culture that any possibilities of such a transformation lie most readily available. Or are we content to dismiss the millions who patronise 'the heritage' as helplessly manipulated subjects of the culture industry, one-dimensional replicants tastelessly consuming the commodified products of a reified society, to be redeemed from cultural degeneracy only by the critical potency of high culture?

At one time the Southwark Globe might have represented such a possibility; but current developments suggest otherwise. One of the 'Midsummer (1991) Events' arranged to advance the ISGC's fund-raising appeal is a performance on the Globe site of *The Tempest* by Phoebus' Cart, a company established by RSC actor Mark Rylance.[29] The production is part of a series of three performances, programmed to take place at three significant sites: Rollright Stones, a megalithic ring in Oxfordshire, Corfe Castle, a National Trust property in Dorset and the site of the Globe reconstruction. The connection between the three sites is far from fortuitous. 'Why', asks the programme, 'were the Globe, the Rose, and the Hope all built in a straight line opposite Ludgate Hill with a design that some say was fashioned on Stonehenge?' The purpose of linking the sites through Shakespeare's play is also candidly described; 'With the help of Shakespeare's gentle magic we hope to re-kindle one of the original functions of these mysterious sites; a celebration of marriage between ourselves and the sky and land we live in' (Rylance himself was married – to a woman – in the centre of the Rollright Ring at a Winter Solstice). The programme conveniently supplies, for cross-reference with the dates of performance, the phases of the moon and the date (11 July) of the 'midsummer festival of joy'. The performances of the play are linked with a series of seminars, given by Rylance's philosophical mentor Peter Dawkins ('a specialist and consultant on the Temple Science, which includes a practical knowledge of earth energies, cosmology, geomancy and sacred architecture') with such titles as 'The Freemasonic and Rosicrucian Mysteries in *The Tempest*', and 'St Alban, Rosicrucian Founder of Modern Freemasonry'. Earth energies are a key concern of Rylance himself: 'Some kinds of activity at these spots helps restore the balance of the earth … I wanted some kind of ceremonial ritual or event that would draw a community to the circle again.'[30] Between Rosicrucianism, Freemasonry, ley lines, the phases of the moon, sacred sites and Shakespeare, the International Shakespeare Globe Centre clearly holds our heritage in safe hands.

CHAPTER SIX

Shakespeare's England (1997)

(WITH ANDREW MURPHY)

ॐ

> It is not easy to discover from what cause the acrimony of a scho-
> liast can naturally proceed. The subjects that may be discussed by
> him are of very small importance; they involve neither property
> nor liberty; nor favour the interest of sect or party.[1]

SO SAMUEL JOHNSON wrote in the introduction to his
edition of Shakespeare. Whatever the applicability of Johnson's sense of the role and importance of the scholar (and, more
particularly, of the literary critic and textual editor) to the world
of the century in which he himself wrote, clearly, in the closing
years of our own century, the business of scholarship has come to
be seen as being of very particular importance, precisely because
it has, in recent years, been viewed as involving crucial issues of
liberty, and of being very deeply furrowed by what Johnson terms
'the interest(s) of sect(s) or part(ies)'. As a result, the academy has
become something of a battleground for competing ideological
positions. In the USA, for instance, conservative commentators
such as Allan Bloom have imagined a left-wing hegemony within
the academic realm which threatens the very future of civilisation
as we know it.[2] In the UK, the conflict has been played out in an
even more public arena, as the schoolteachers' professional
organisations have endeavoured, over a long period of time, to
resist the efforts of the Conservative government to refashion
the educational system according to its own image, re-imposing
on English teachers and their students notions of, for instance,
canonicity and 'standard English'.

It is English, indeed, which has been at the centre of so many of these disputes encompassing the political and academic realms. Terry Eagleton once wrote of the enormous self-centralising power of an emergent new criticism that 'in the early 1920s it was desperately unclear why English was worth studying at all; by the early 1930s it had become a question of why it was worth wasting your time on anything else'.³ One might wonder, of course, whether this is still true for *students* today, but, at any rate, the discipline of English seems of late to be attracting a very great deal of attention from politicians and their attendant satellites. A particularly good example of this new centrality of English could be seen at the 1993 Conservative Party conference in the UK, when the British Prime Minister, John Major, in the midst of his annual keynote address to the party faithful, took the time to launch a counter-attack against a group of some five hundred academics who had published a letter in the British press condemning the government's policies on the study of literature. Mr Major, waving a copy of the letter in the air, and pledging to speak to such academics in a language of which they themselves might approve, declared resolutely: 'Me and my party ain't going to take what them on the left says is OK. Right?'⁴

The letter in question had addressed, among other things, the issue of how and when Shakespeare should be taught in British schools, with the original writers of the letter registering their opposition to the government's policy that the study of Shakespeare should be a mandatory part of the curriculum for students from an early age.⁵ Shakespeare, indeed, has always been of centrally strategic importance in the battleground formed by the intersection of education and politics. In August 1993, the British Sunday newspaper *The Observer* ran a lengthy feature article in its Review section under the headline '"Presume not that I am the thing I was"' and subtitled 'The battle of the Bard'. In this article, the journalist Peter Watson traces the rise, within Shakespeare studies, of the related critical strategies of new historicism and cultural materialism and charts the reactions which these approaches have provoked among conservative critics. 'The battle and the bitchiness are far from over', Watson writes, 'the Bard is still up for grabs.'[6] It is the contention, of course, of many scholars that 'the Bard' has, in fact, always been up for grabs. Since the first wave of British cultural materialist Shakespeare criticism redrew the theoretical map in the mid-1980s, subsequent writers – in particular Gary Taylor in *Reinventing Shakespeare*, Michael Bristol in *Shakespeare's America, America's Shakespeare*, and Jean Marsden in *The Appropriation of Shakespeare* – have produced cultural histories of the ways in which Shakespeare has, ever since the seventeenth century, been constituted and reconstituted, fashioned and refashioned to serve political and ideological ends – on both sides of the Atlantic.[7] Those who accuse radical critics of somehow 'misappropriating' Shakespeare for their own nefarious ends thus fail to see that Shakespeare has always been the subject of appropriations of one sort or another. Indeed, we will recall that in the dramatist's own lifetime his work was deployed for explicitly political ends on at least one occasion, when the supporters of the Earl of Essex commissioned a special performance of *Richard II* on the eve of their rebellion against Elizabeth in 1601.

But, of course, we might also question in this context the conservative assumption that there does in fact exist in the work of Shakespeare something coherent, stable and unitary which is *capable* of being 'mis'appropriated by the cultural materialists. Conversely, this can, in turn, be restored to an original pristine self, if only the defacing graffiti of a radical critical practice could be expunged from its surface. It is not just a matter of interrogating the conservative assumption that there is a transcendent and universal meaning which inheres in the works of Shakespeare, a meaning to which we must somehow 'return', eschewing the wilful 'mis'reading of the radicals. We must also interrogate the prior assumption which lies behind this conservative view: that the works themselves constitute a unitary and coherent set of entities, whose material stability is safely to be taken for granted.

~ↄ

Such a confidence in the unity and stability, both of 'Shakespeare' and of the Shakespeare text, certainly lies at the heart of conservative thinking as it manifests itself in promotion of the British Government's 'National Curriculum for English'. Shakespeare, according to the proponents of the National Curriculum, remains indispensable because he is central to the 'literary heritage'. According to this view there exists something of value, literature, that descends from the past and is inherited in the present. Although the object of value is a common inheritance, theoretically available to us all, not everyone who is entitled to claim it does actually do so. From this idea derives the concept of the National Curriculum as an 'enabling curriculum', facilitating access to their inheritance for those who would otherwise remain disinherited.

Shakespeare, together with a strikingly narrow range of Victorian and Edwardian classics, represents this literary heritage in exemplary form. In 1992 British secondary schools were required to ensure (at absurdly short notice) that 14-year-olds would study one of three prescribed Shakespeare plays (*Julius Caesar*, *A Midsummer Night's Dream* and *Romeo and Juliet*), and be tested on what they had studied. So your heritage does not come to you automatically, any more than do state benefits or the contents of a will: you are required to prove your title to that inheritance in exactly the same way (via the system of *probate*, a term derived from the Latin *probare*, to test or prove) as you have to prove your title to private property.

The process by which your inheritance can be claimed, as the metaphor begins to disclose its true contents, is therefore less about possession and more about establishing entitlement; less of a free bequest and more about requirement, imposition, testing and proof. 'English' is in this way used in much the same way as Latin was used in the British grammar school system: to assess levels of cultural competence; to identify those who are worthy of the literary heritage, and to differentiate them from those who are patently unfit to inherit. The crucial difference is, of course, that Latin as employed in the grammar school system was a dead language, a specifically literary rather than an oral form, which even in the time of its currency bore an oblique relation to its own equivalent vernacular; and which naturally bore a precisely negative relation to the contemporary vernacular within which it operated (indeed still operates) in grammar schools. Contemporary English is a language in use, in continual exchange and change: dynamic and developing and adapting to new relations of cultural exchange as new social and political relations evolve. Moreover, there is not, of course, only one English, but many: class and regional dialects and all the Englishes of the large anglophone world. In terms of the population of Britain itself, English has long co-existed with other languages such as Welsh and Gaelic, and with the languages of all the other language groups that make up the global population of a multi-cultural society. The difficulties entailed in using this language, as an equivalent of Latin, to express and embody standards of linguistic acquisition and performance will be self-evident.

This problem is solved by the privileging of one form of English, a particular class-dialect, as the dominant form: standard English. Standard English, the educated language of the ruling class, derived from a particular regional dialect of early English, is now declared the universal lingua franca of all classes, races and creeds. Standard English, though 'owned' in terms both of speech and writing by a privileged few, is none the less nominally available to all: a common inheritance, a universal right. Standard English may not be the language you learn 'naturally' from family and immediate social environment but it is there as a linguistic standard to which you may aspire, promising the rewards of intelligibility, freedom of speech and communication, educational and social advancement.

Standard English is also declared the common language of the literary inheritance; the language of the Bible and of Shakespeare: a language exemplifying a cultural continuity through the process of historical and political change. We who speak the tongue that Shakespeare spake (sorry, spoke) enter in that process of linguistic transaction a cultural continuum continually demonstrated by the palpable contemporary existence of the literary heritage.

The key ideas outlined here are all linked in an ideological ensemble purporting to represent a coherent, organically unified cultural 'core'. The literary heritage, based upon a notion of classic writing narrowly selected from a vast range of possibilities, and including an indispensable, unavoidable component – Shakespeare – is made possible and exemplified by standard English, the universal dialect of a linguistic and literary common inheritance. Language acquisition and literary education are seen as a seamless continuum, each an inevitable condition of the other. Literary and linguistic competence, demonstrable via certain media of academic performance, can be tested against the same measurable performance indicators. The ability to speak and write, clearly and confidently, standard English; and the capacity to demonstrate an acceptable level of understanding vis-à-vis Shakespearean drama, are in the National Curriculum system regarded as interdependent and reliably measurable by common criteria. In order to speak the tongue that Shakespeare spake/spoke, we are obliged to frequent the writing which embodies that speech.

But much of our 'literary heritage', including the work of the one writer regarded as indispensable, was, of course, written long before the invention of standard English. The process of systemising the English language, establishing principles of correctness in relation to its grammar and syntax, determining conventions of regularity in relation to spelling and punctuation, which can be said to have commenced in the eighteenth century, was not accomplished, and certainly not disseminated through the educational system, before the nineteenth. Early modern English, the English of the sixteenth and seventeenth centuries, was in many ways quite unlike standard English: in some ways more systematic – enjoying, for example, a much wider range of usable grammatical forms than those available to modern standard English – and in some ways, especially in relation to spelling and punctuation, far less regularised. The continuing availability into the seventeenth century of Latin as a medium of writing indicates that English had not at that stage of its development achieved complete cultural dominance. English was still sufficiently 'emergent' as a language for its written usage to be closely linked with the linguistic variety of the vernacular.

Shakespeare's English was therefore very obviously a non standard English, both structurally and contextually very different from its modern counterpart. It had a different grammatical system, different rules of spelling and punctuation; a different set of relations between written and spoken language and a different relationship, among the educated classes, with other languages. English was in that early modern period a dynamic and developing language, characterised by diversity and change, the very opposite of a fixed, regularised and systematised form such as standard English. Indeed the historical and political processes that made standard English possible and necessary – the emergence from medieval Catholic Europe of England/Britain as an independent national state, and the eventual rise of that state to imperial domination – were only just beginning. In the plays of Marlowe, Shakespeare and their contemporaries English is frequently marked off from other languages, other regional and class-dialects, as a distinct linguistic medium: but that evidence of linguistic differentiation only indicates that the process of shaping within the language a national identity was at an early stage of development.

How is it possible then to use the work of an early modern dramatist, written long before the language was regulated and codified into what we now know as standard English, to exemplify that linguistic form? Simply, the answer is, by translation. Even a cursory glance at a manuscript record or printed text from the early modern period would be sufficient to convince the reader that the writing of that period does not exemplify standard English usage. But this incontrovertible documentary evidence is, of course, not normally available to the modern reader – often not even to the university student of literature, and certainly not to the school student reading a Shakespeare play within the context of the National Curriculum for English – since Shakespeare is not read in early modern English, but in modern 'translation'.

Many modern readers of Shakespeare, particularly younger readers, lulled by long-established editorial traditions into an implicit confidence in the object of their attention, probably have little idea of what a sixteenth-century printed play text actually looked like. Confronted with an example, she or he could be forgiven for recoiling before the intimidating display of linguistic and visual strangeness – antique type, non-standardised spelling, archaic orthographic conventions, unfamiliar and irregular speech prefixes, oddly placed stage directions, and possibly an absence of act and scene divisions. 'It looks more like Chaucer than Shakespeare,' said one sixth-former, presented with a facsimile of an Elizabethan text, nearly calling attention to the peculiar elisions by which Shakespeare is accepted as modern, while Chaucer is categorised as ancient. Yet Shakespeare too is read in modernised forms. A student reading Chaucer in modern translation knows that the text is a contemporary version, not a historical document. But the modern translations of Shakespeare which universally pass as accurate and authentic representations of an original – the standard editions – offer themselves simultaneously as historical document and accessible modern version, like a tidily restored ancient building.

The standard modern editions of Shakespeare, much more obviously compatible with the conventions of modern standard English than the original printed texts, thus operate continually to foster the illusion that these writings of the late sixteenth and early seventeenth centuries effortlessly prefigured the grammatical system, syntactical conventions, rules of spelling and punctuation characteristic of standard English. The modern Shakespeare edition thus seems anachronistically to exemplify that standard English that was invented centuries after the initial production and performance of the plays. With its regularisation of spelling and punctuation, together with editorial systematisation of whatever appears 'irregular' in the original texts (whether that be a matter of grammar, stage directions, structural divisions into act and scene), the standard modern edition presents to the reader a Shakespeare which, smoothly translated into a familiar modern idiom, seems to present far fewer problems of comprehension even for the relatively unsophisticated reader. The modernised edition of Shakespeare thus performs an essential service to the National Curriculum. By completing the continuum of language and literature, speech and writing, past and present, and enabling a transhistorical 'Shakespeare', purged of all disconcerting historical difference, it stands as an incontrovertible demonstration of the 'greatness' embodied in 'English' – whether that nomenclature is employed to signify a literature, a language, a culture or a political state.

Inheriting Shakespeare through the National Curriculum, we may well feel disposed to believe that, as fortunate beneficiaries of a generous bequest, we have come into possession of a valuable antique. But barely concealed beneath the patina of antiquity we can discern the varnish of novelty. This is not an antique but an imitation, perfectly adapted to the conveniences of modern living: 'repro Shakespeare'.

⚬

When the British Education Secretary insists that schoolchildren be compelled to read Shakespeare, the presumption that there exists such a thing as a coherent 'Shakespeare text' for them to read is manifestly demonstrated by the unassailed supremacy of the modern edition. British schoolchildren and their teachers are spoilt for choice of such texts, as is evidenced by the recent publication of a volume entitled *Which Shakespeare?* This is a sort of 'consumer's guide' to the major available editions of Shakespeare's plays, which aims to assist the teacher and scholar in making an informed choice among competing flocks of Penguins, Bantams, Signets, Ardens, Cambridges and Oxfords.[8] All these editions of Shakespeare are much the same. Or rather, they are simultaneously the same and yet not the same. The texts of Shakespeare commonly available in major editions differ little enough from each other in substance, because they have all been produced under the guiding principles of a textual theory which came into prominence among editors of early modern texts in the early decades of the twentieth century – a theory derived in the first instance from the realm of biblical studies. What these texts do differ from (and often differ from very significantly indeed) is the texts of the same plays as they were first published during Shakespeare's own lifetime, or in the years immediately following his death in 1616.

The text, then, the government would have the British schoolchild read is, in fact, not a text that would have been familiar to Shakespeare's own contemporaries. Take the instance of *Hamlet.* Three texts of a play with that name somewhere in the title (and all attributed to Shakespeare as author) were published within two decades of each other at the beginning of the seventeenth century: individual quarto editions in 1603 and 1604/5 (Q1 and Q2 respectively) and the First Folio text of 1623 (F), as part of Heminge and Condell's edition of the collected works of Shakespeare. All three texts differ substantially from each other. Q1 is a short text, comprising some 2,200 lines. Q2 is the longest version, yielding approximately 3,800 lines. F is about 230 lines shorter than Q2, but also includes some seventy lines not present in that text. But *Hamlet,* in fact, provides just one example of the convoluted history of the process of transmission of Shakespeare's texts. Many of the other plays are equally problematic, and problematic in different ways. The first publication of *The Taming of the Shrew,* for instance, was in the 1623 Folio collection. But almost three decades earlier, in 1594, a play entitled *The Taming of a Shrew* had appeared in print, with no authorial attribution offered on the title page. The relationship between the two texts is complex and, finally, indeterminate: '*A Shrew* has sometimes been regarded as the source for *The Shrew;* some scholars have believed that both plays derive independently from an earlier play, now lost; it has even been suggested that Shakespeare wrote both plays.'9

Where, then, in all of this, is the body of the individual Shakespeare play? How do we deal with this proliferation of early modern Shakespeares? In the opening decades of the present century, the new bibliographers, building on the work of such eighteenth-century Shakespeare editors as Edward Capell and Edmond Malone, essayed a solution to these problems.10 Drawing on theories of textual transmission developed in the realm of biblical studies by scholars such as Karl Lachmann, the proponents of the new bibliography foregrounded a narrative of textual history that posited a stable, coherent authorial text which had been 'corrupted' in the process of entering the printed state. The morally charged lexicon of the new bibliographers is perhaps not so surprising, given the original provenance of the theories which they deployed. For example, in *Textual and Literary Criticism,* Fredson Bowers writes:

> The most important concern of the textual bibliographer is to guard the purity of the important basic documents of our literature and culture. This is a matter of principle on which there can be no compromise. One can no more permit 'just a little corruption' to pass unheeded in the transmission of our literary heritage than 'just a little sin' was possible in Eden.11

The new bibliographers seemed to regard the printed state of a text as a sort of post-lapsarian realm – to be born into print was in some sense necessarily to carry a stigma of corruption. The objective of the new bibliographers was to save such fallen texts

and restore them to the wholesome state they had been in immediately when their authors' hands had finished fashioning them.
In the process, the wayward text is retrieved and restored to
something akin to a state of grace.

The views of the new bibliographers have had a profound
impact on the practice of textual editing. The effect of the
deployment of their theories in the editing of Shakespeare has led
to the raising of relatively uniform and unitary editions from the
multiplicity and polyvocality of original texts from which these
modern editions have been compiled. Where multiple contemporary editions of a play exist (as they do in the case of some nine-
teen plays from the Shakespeare canon), the individual
contemporary texts have been sorted, and subjected to a process
of conflation and consolidation, whereby a particular copy text is
added to (and, sometimes, subtracted from) in order to arrive at
the best possible text. As Bowers puts it: 'the immediate concern
of textual bibliography is only to recover as exactly as may be the
form of the text directly underneath the printed copy.'[12]

One problem with this approach is that 'the text directly
underneath the printed copy' is entirely notional, since, in Shakespeare's case, none of these manuscript texts has survived.[13] So
the conflationary endeavour is an exercise in attempting to get
back to an ideal 'original', but an original of which no direct
knowledge can ever be possible. As we have noted elsewhere:

> The object of which we can have direct knowledge, the printed
> text, is judged to be corrupt by conjectural reference to the object
> of which we can by definition have no direct knowledge, the
> uncorrupted (but non-existent) manuscript. The procedure is
> self-contradictory, since the historical document is being com-
> pared with an 'original' that can be speculatively constructed only
> from the evidence of the historical document itself.[14]

The new bibliographic enterprise has been criticised on other
grounds also. It presumes, for instance, that, given a set of diverse
early modern editions of a particular play, the editor's task is to

discover among those texts a single set of 'correct' readings which
can (and must) be privileged above all other possibilities. If a line
or a speech or an entire scene exists in two or more versions, the
editor labours to determine which is the correct form of the text –
which is, in Charlton Hinman's words, 'the most authoritative
possible [text] of Shakespeare', which is his definitive version 'just
as he meant [it] to stand'.[15] Editing becomes, within this regime,
an extended process of separating the textual sheep from the textual goats and of shepherding back into the control text any stray
sheep which may have wandered off and turned up in the
chronologically neighbouring fields of another edition. This
process precludes the possibility that more than one reading may,
in fact, be admissible. As Gary Taylor writes in *William Shakespeare: A Textual Companion*, under these circumstances, 'faced
with two sheep, it is all too easy to insist that one must be a
goat'.[16]

Centring the business of textual production on a single unitary figure called 'Shakespeare' serves to obscure the institutional
history of the production and dissemination of those texts which
are united under his name. Ironically, both the new bibliographers and the Oxford editors have been among those who have
placed much emphasis on the excavation and bringing to prominence of the material and institutional conditions of the texts that
they have edited. In *On Editing Shakespeare and the Elizabethan
Dramatists*, for example, Fredson Bowers contrasts the materialist
approach of the bibliographer with the 'unscientific' efforts of the
literary critic:

> Bibliography may be said to attack textual problems from the
> mechanical point of view, using evidence which must deliberately
> avoid being coloured by literary considerations. Non-bibliograph-
> ical textual criticism works with meanings and literary values. If
> these last are divorced from all connections with the evidence of
> the mechanical process that imprinted meaningful symbols on a
> sheet of paper, no check-rein of fact or probability can restrain the
> farthest reaches of idle speculation.[17]

In this spirit the new bibliographers initiated the field of 'compositor study', meticulously combing through texts in an effort to unravel the history of, for example, the passage of the First Folio through William and Isaac Jaggard's printing house.[18] Likewise, Wells and Taylor have laid great emphasis on the theatrical context of the plays, stressing their function as performance scripts.[19]

The ultimate effect of such work has been, however, to constellate the material conditions of production, distribution and performance around the unitary figure of Shakespeare, or rather, more accurately, to establish a hierarchy of production and dissemination with Shakespeare at the summit, as the overweening source of meaning and authority. This can be seen, for instance, in the approach of W.W. Greg to the interrelation of the different hands participating in the manuscript copy of *Sir Thomas More*. Hand D, it has been suggested, belongs to Shakespeare. Hand C (which, as it happens, bears a strong resemblance to Hand D) 'worked over various parts of the manuscript, stitching together passages from the others, copying ... correcting some stage directions, and getting the thing into shape for the actors to work on'.[20] Greg cast Hand C as 'playhouse functionary' and, as Scott McMillin has observed:

> The model that produces this distinction is the model of literary canonisation, which gives the privilege of genius to authors and holds those responsible for the material conditions of literature – actors, for example, but also printers, scribes, stationers, and paper manufacturers, just to name those whose work Shakespeare would have valued – as more or less contemptible.[21]

By contrast with this approach, an alternative view of the process of literary production has been advanced by Jerome J. McGann, initially in his 1983 *Critique of Modern Textual Criticism*. In the *Critique* McGann advances what has since come to be characterised as a 'social theory of texts', arguing that 'Authority is a social nexus, not a personal possession; and if the authority for specific literary works is initiated anew for each work by some specific artists, its initiation takes place in a necessary and integral historical environment of great complexity.'[22] In *The Textual Condition*, McGann further observes that 'texts are produced and reproduced under specific social and institutional conditions, and hence ... every text, including those that may appear to be purely private, is a social text'.[23] McGann thus stresses the inextricable interlacing of the author into a greater social matrix. In McGann's model, the social nexus serves collaboratively in the process of generating and disseminating meaning, in contrast to the traditional view which would see the author as the unique source of a meaning that is carried by the channels of production and distribution, acting merely as subordinate agents of transmission.

Of course, McGann, as a textual critic writing his *Critique* in the early 1980s, was advancing a theory of authorship and authority which, while at odds with the views of many of his colleagues in the world of textual scholarship, would have been perfectly intelligible to other contemporary literary theorists. Some fifteen years before the *Critique* appeared in print, Roland Barthes had proclaimed, in 'The death of the author', that 'to give a text an Author is to impose a limit on that text, to furnish it with a final signified, to close the writing'.[24] Foucault also interrogated the concept of authorship and the privileging and centralising of the author with regard to the text in his seminal essay 'What is an author?' Like Barthes, Foucault saw the invocation of the concept of the author essentially as the deployment of a strategy of containment, whereby meaning is delimited, divided and constrained: 'the author does not precede the works; he is a certain functional principle by which, in our culture, one limits, excludes, and chooses; in short, by which one impedes the free circulation, the free manipulation, the free composition, decomposition, and recomposition of fiction.'[25]

The pertinence of these remarks to the field of traditional Shakespeare editing should be readily apparent. For the new bibliographers, faced with a plurality of texts all purporting to be incarnations of a single particular work, the objective was to discover within their dispersed parts the single coherent text which Shakespeare truly intended. Once this ideal text was arrived at, all other meanings were to be rigorously excluded. The revisionists, by contrast, admitted the possibility of multiple versions and of a plurality of meanings, but they insisted on always referring this multiplicity to the unifying figure of Shakespeare, as the single source of the texts' polyvocality. In the case of both the new bibliographers and the revisionists Shakespeare becomes precisely what Foucault has characterised as a functional principle of limitation, exclusion and choice: Shakespeare is engaged as a means of limiting the field of potential readings, excluding from the set of available meanings those which are deemed not to be truly 'authorial'.

☙

> That which withers in the age of mechanical reproduction is the aura of the work of art … the technique of reproduction detaches the reproduced object from the domain of tradition. By making many reproductions it substitutes a plurality of copies for a unique existence.[26]

It is a mark of the essential unity of approach of the new bibliographers and the revisionists that the latter, while setting themselves up in opposition to their bibliographic predecessors, should have accepted virtually without question certain of the new bibliographers' foundational assumptions, including, most notably, the sorting of the earliest Shakespeare texts into sets of 'good' and 'bad' quartos.[27] The 'good' quartos are those which can be considered 'authentically' 'Shakespearean'. By contrast the 'bad' quartos are characterised as being imperfect, pirated copies of the true Shakespeare originals (patched together, in the narrative of 'memorial construction', from memory by actors who had participated in performances of the plays).[28] As long ago as 1982, Random Cloud (Randall McLeod) criticised this practice of sort-

ing texts into morally charged categories, observing in 'The marriage of good and bad Quartos' that 'employing moral categories
in textual work obliges one to choose: to reject Evil once and for
all, and to strike out toward Goodness (and toward Shakespeare,
who is a Good writer)'.[29] McLeod registers here the imposition of
constraints on the greater circulation of meaning which Foucault
sees as being characteristic of the author function generally. The
invocation of the concept of authorial authenticity serves as a
principle for privileging one set of texts, to the exclusion of others.

Jonathan Goldberg has noted the intersection of the concerns
of post-revisionist textual theorists with the parameters of the
general post-structuralist project, observing that 'post-structuralism and the new textual criticism coincide, historically – and
theoretically. Both have called the criterion of authorial intention
into question, thereby detaching the supposed sovereign author
from texts open to and constituted by a variety of interventions.'[30] The implications of this intersection have yet to be fully
appreciated. A clear imperative view now exists for the working
through of a new conception of editorial and critical practice in
the light of this interconnected theoretical framework. If we are
indeed to pursue the pathway which Goldberg charts as the
'detaching [of] the supposed sovereign author from texts open to
and constituted by a variety of interventions', then clearly we
must break not only from the conflationary texts of the new bibliographers but also from the author-centred texts of the revisionists. This requires the abandonment of such morally charged
notions as the division of the kingdom of writing into good and
bad texts. In the case of the 'Shakespeare' canon, all the relevant
texts must be opened up to analytical scrutiny, as historical documents of interest and importance in their own right.[31]

To propose turning attention to these texts is not to call for a
Boweresque redemptive mission whereby the bad quartos, having
long fallen by the wayside, will now be lifted up into glory. Nor is
the point of the exercise to reverse the value judgement tradition-

ally passed on these texts by suggesting that, far from being 'bad' texts, they are, in fact, just as good as their supposedly authentic fellows. The point is, rather, to move *beyond* the application of the criterion of value to the project of literary scholarship, and to continue the process, most recently foregrounded by new historicism/cultural materialism, of questioning the very notion of a category of literature which is distinct and separable from all other forms of writing.[32]

We have come a long way, then, from the letter-waving, jeering-demotic assurance of the British Prime Minister and his Cabinet colleagues, who would insist on making Shakespeare a mandatory part of every British schoolchild's education. For the 'Battle of the Bard' entails more than just a debate over the ways in which Shakespeare may (or may not) be interpreted, but extends to the question of what constitutes not just that centralising force labelled Shakespeare but also the very materiality of the texts united under that identity.

As a final thought, we might do well to remember that politicians are, in any case, notoriously liable to be caught wrong-footed when it comes to invoking Shakespeare. In the Clarence Thomas confirmation hearings in the USA in 1992, one of the senators on the committee set up to examine the allegations of sexual harassment brought against Thomas by his former co-worker, Anita Hill, proclaimed, for the benefit of the committee, a recitation of the 'Good name in man and woman' speech from *Othello*, apparently unaware that the speech was that of a character described in the 'Names of the Actors' in the First Folio as 'a Villaine'. Perhaps he, like his counterparts in the UK, should have read his texts of *Othello* more carefully.

PART THREE

Myth

CHAPTER SEVEN

Bardolatry (1988)

ᔆᕀ

Stratford will help you to understand Shakespeare.
F .J. Furnivall[1]

I N T H E S P R I N G of 1936 the Directors of the Stratford-upon-Avon Festival Company received the following cable: *'Please send earth Shakespeare's garden water River Avon for dedication Shakespeare Theatre, Dallas, Texas, July 1st'*. The 'Shakespeare Theatre' referred to was a 'replica' of the Globe playhouse erected for the Great Texas Fair; it had previously served as the centrepiece of a mock 'English village' constructed for the World's Fair in Chicago. Stratford knew how to respond to what might seem to us a bizarre request. A group of citizens and actors gathered in the garden of Shakespeare's birthplace to meet the American Vice-Consul. In a solemn ceremony a handful of that rich dust was disinterred and placed with ritual formality into a small box made of charred wood – a relic from the Shakespeare Memorial Theatre which burned down in 1926. The party then repaired to the premises of the Stratford rowing club on the banks of the Avon. Mr Fordham Flower, descendant of the brewing family which endowed the Shakespeare Memorial Theatre, accompanied the Vice-Consul on a small raft to the middle of the river. Into the sacred stream they dipped a small bottle made of aluminium (light metal, like brewing, being an important local industry) and bearing Shakespeare's coat-of-arms. Both sacred earth and holy water were conveyed to New York, free of carriage charges, by the

Cunard Line: thence to Dallas, where in a ritual of libation the *ersatz* Globe was consecrated by the sprinkling of Stratford earth and Avon water; and the superflux exposed to the general veneration of Dallas.[2]

⤬

These rites, based on an attenuated form of relic-worship, are the liturgical properties of a religion: bardolatry, the worship of Shakespeare. Visitors to the Great Texas Fair in 1936, as they watched the pageant of Queen Elizabeth I and her morris dancers, and were ushered into the replica Globe for a severely truncated performance of a Shakespeare play (the forty-five minutes traffic of that particular stage)[3] were invited into communion with a ritual enacting an idealised English past: a past linked to the present in transnational and transcontinental continuity, by the power of these vatic, totemic images.

Though there were a few isolated prophets, bardolatry as an organised evangelical movement scarcely existed before David Garrick's Stratford jubilee in 1769. Crowds followed the corpse of Ben Jonson to Westminster on his death in 1637, and Francis Beaumont was thought to deserve a place in the Abbey; Shakespeare had been laid to rest in 1616 in a relatively little, obscure grave in the chancel of Stratford church. He was not even eligible for a place there on the strength of his poetry or theatrical achievement but as a local landowner and lessee of tithes.[4] (In 1623 Puritan-tinged Stratford corporation paid Shakespeare's company, the King's Men, not to perform in the Guildhall)[5]. Nonetheless, by the mid-eighteenth century Stratford was certainly the centre for some kind of tourist industry, run by some pretty unscrupulous local entrepreneurs.[6] In the garden of New Place, the house Shakespeare bought and lived in on his retirement, the famous mulberry tree, reputed (by an aptly named Thomas Sharp) to have been planted by the Bard's own hand, had certainly acquired by this period sufficient sacrosanctity to form

'Here's Flowers for you ... ': Beer mat from the Bard's local
brewery. *Reproduced by kind permission of Whitbread Flowers*

an object of tourist interest and attraction.[7] In 1756 the Rev. Francis William Gastrell, an irascible cleric who had acquired the property, was so exasperated by 'the frequent importunities of travellers', and so annoyed with the tree itself (an object of hoary and ancient growth which was engendering rising damp in the walls of his house) that he had it chopped down; whereupon it very quickly began, like the wood of the true cross, to increase and multiply into innumerable relics and souvenirs.[8] This legendary product of Bardic husbandry soon became available from all good local craftshops in the form of 'many curious toys and useful articles'.[9] In 1759 Gastrell knocked the house down as well, and thus entered history as one of the great cultural vandals.[10]

Another Stratford entrepreneur and founder of the tourist

industry was John Jordan, who set up a rival trade in curios from
the wood of a crab-apple tree under which Shakespeare (who
was, according to beer mats supplied by Flowers' brewery,
'extremely fond of drinking hearty draughts of English ale') was
reputed to have lapsed into unconsciousness during a pub-
crawl.[11] John Ward's anecdote, describing Shakespeare's death
from the consequences of a piss-up with Drayton and Ben Jonson, neglects to mention what was being drunk at the time: and
there seems to be no other evidence of Shakespeare's bibulous
preferences. But by this period the Stratford brewing trade was
sufficiently well established to retrospectively determine the
Bard's particular tipple, and to connect in a single commercial
dimension the diverse products of local business enterprise.

❦

This was the great age of forgery and fabrication in the Shakespeare industry, and Stratford was the site of a great deal of
healthy commercial competition. Jordan, for example, ridiculed
the pretensions of 'the Birthplace' in Henley Street to authenticity, calling it 'a most flagrant and gross imposition';[12] and it was
Jordan also who decided that the house known as 'Mary Arden's
house' at Wilmcote was the domicile of Shakespeare's mother.
The attribution is an arbitrary fantasy: but along with the Birthplace, New Place, Hall's Croft and Anne Hathaway's Cottage,
Mary Arden's house occupies its place as a station on the route of
bardolatrous pilgrimage.

By 1800 the Birthplace was partly a butcher's shop and partly
an inn called the Swan and Maidenhead,[13] a sign replete with
romantic connotations for the devotees of Queen Gloriana and
the Sweet Swan of Avon. Here, as Ivor Brown observed, it was
possible to get Bed, Board and Bard under one roof: but the sign
itself was taken down and deconstructed in 1808 by a company of
drunken Warwickshire yeomanry who felt it inappropriate that
the only maidenhead left intact in Stratford should be a wooden

one. The butcher's shop was then occupied by a Mrs Hornby, who traded in bardolatry as well as bacon by exhibiting a collection of relics, including a legendary piece of furniture reported to be Shakespeare's own chair. Curiouser and curio-ser, the chair was fabulous in more senses than one: although every visitor paid to cut a piece off, it never grew any smaller. A rival widow who actually owned the building then took over the pub, and decided to evict Widow Hornby and appropriate the bardolatrous trade for herself. Widow Hornby decamped, but took her relics with her, and set up in competition in a house across the road. 'These rival dowagers', a contemporary witness records, 'parted on envious terms; they were constantly to be seen at each others' doors abusing each other and their respective visitors, and frequently with so much acerbity as to disgust and even deter the latter from entering either dwelling'.[14]

These images of nineteenth-century Stratford appropriately map the contours of the Shakespeare myth: an atmosphere of unscrupulous opportunism, commercial exploitation and gross imposture; the *laissez-faire* environment of a cultural industry in which the free play of market forces determines all values. The reverential Victorian pilgrim journeying to Stratford in search of a quasi-religious communion with a more settled, more tranquil, more certain past, found himself instead caught in the crossfire of a Widows' War, and probably felt disposed to wish a plague on both their houses. You could wander through medieval streets and observe Tudor buildings: but the *values* you came in search of – truth, authenticity, the assurance and consolation of a vanished golden age, the transcendent illumination of transhistorical genius – were not after all to be discovered, visibly embedded in an uninterrupted continuum of time and space, like fossils in the strata of rocks. The past itself was the site of a furious battle between competing appropriators, rival enterprises within a cultural industry.

⁓

The cultural and commercial antagonisms of the Victorian period were ultimately reconciled by the formation of a monopolistic
organisation, the Shakespeare Birthplace Trust, which now represents the authentic clerisy of the Shakespeare religion: Stratford
itself its church, and its high priest Dr Levi Fox. No fraudulent
claims are now made, no original chairs or pieces of mulberry
tree sold in local souvenir shops. Stratford contains, as well as the
'Shakespearean Properties' and innumerable commercial
adjuncts to the tourist industry, the Royal Shakespeare Theatre,
country home of the most prestigious British theatre company,
and the Shakespeare Centre, a highly respected research institute.
Tourism is regarded by some serious (and some cynical) scholars
and theatrical practitioners as the bread-and-butter trade on
which the more elevated superstructures of culture can be erected, in an age when State subsidy of the arts and education is that
much harder to come by.[15] How then are these cults and rituals
of bardolatry to be understood in the present? What relation do
they have, if any, to the position of Shakespeare within the apparatus of British culture?

Tourists are still lured to Stratford by the deployment of an
overtly religious language of pilgrimage and worship. 'It is the
fame of the properties associated with William Shakespeare and
his family, that makes Stratford-upon-Avon a Mecca for visitors
from all over the world', writes Levi Fox in the current guidebook.[16] 'Anne Hathaway's cottage, the home of Shakespeare's wife
before her marriage, is one of England's most famous buildings.
The reason is not far to seek. Apart from its literary and romantic
associations as the scene of Shakespeare's youthful courtship, it is
a property of outstanding architectural appeal which for generations has been a shrine of international literary pilgrimage.' A 1951
guidebook to Anne Hathaway's cottage was confident that *As
You Like It* contains an 'unmistakable reference' to this cottage,
in Celia's lines about their holiday home in the Forest of Arden.[17]
In the current official Stratford guidebook the claim is moderat-
ed, but Levi Fox still preserves its substance: 'it has been suggested

that Shakespeare's description of the situation of Celia's home in *As You Like It* was inspired by the poet's recollections of his wife's early home.' These lines were, of course, originally delivered on a bare, unlocalised stage on London's Bankside. The 'Arden' of the play is the Ardennes of northern France rather than the forest which once existed in Warwickshire and which may or may not have adjoined the cottage in which Anne Hathaway, whom Shakespeare may or may not have married, may or may not have lived. But bardolatry trades in certainty, not in the slippery elusiveness of documentary fact: the buildings have acted as objects of pilgrimage and shrines of worship for generations, and that in itself is an assurance of their value.

And what values are these buildings in practice commandeered to express? Pure, unimpeded images of an idealised historical past. The photographs in the guidebooks appear purified of any association with the complex, sordid present; isolated as timeless symbols of a neat, tidy, innocent world: 'so venerable', as Matthew Arnold said of Oxford, 'so lovely; so unravaged by the fierce intellectual life of the century'. Guidebooks from the 1950s appear to have used pre-war photographs, and one even offered the monuments of Stratford transmuted into the pastel tints of a series of English watercolours. An idealised 'English' past, picturesque and untroubled, is thus embodied and incorporated into commodities for sale to national and international markets, the transaction simultaneously satisfying both cultural and commercial demands. These publications, as Roland Barthes said of the *Blue Guide*, 'answer in fact none of the questions which a modern traveller can ask himself while crossing a countryside which is real *and which exists in time.* To select only monuments suppresses at one stroke the reality of the land and that of its people, it accounts for nothing of the present, that is, nothing historical, and as a consequence, the monuments themselves become undecipherable, therefore senseless'.[18]

❧

The modern tourist, as a growing body of sociological work has shown, is a direct descendant of the medieval pilgrim. Both are engaged in a ritualised passage to a sacred site; both are in search of the icons of their culture: relics, pieces of the true cross, burnished with age but sanctified by the miracle of survival through time. Pilgrims, Donald Horne argues in his fine study *The Great Museum*, were the first mass tourists, and sightseeing and souvenir collecting the inescapable material dimension of their spiritual quest. In marxist terms, tourism is a commercial exchange process whose symbolic centre is the fetishism of objects: and museum relics and treasures can certainly be said to possess such a holy, magical aura.[19]

The symbolic function of a souvenir or photograph is partly acquisitive[20] – you exhibit it to show that you've been there, done that place – but it also operates, like the medieval relic, as the embodiment of an experience: a trigger for memory, with a magical capacity to release recollection; a mnemonic device designed to preserve memory from the wastage of time. In an age of mechanical reproduction, photography familiarises the objects of tourism to such a degree that one wonders why anyone would still want to visit the *Mona Lisa* or the Parthenon or the leaning tower of Pisa at all. Oral tradition is likely to preserve the 'magic' of an unseen place intact; visual tradition (photography) should gradually bleed away that magic, imperceptibly but relentlessly wearing away the sacred aura. Yet in practice the impulse to visit a place in person, to see it with one's own eyes 'as it really is' seems to grow rather than diminish. When we arrive we observe the 'reality' of a place in a context prescribed by visual tradition, 'discovering' that the place is after all synonymous with the photographs; and our own snapshots obediently reproduce the images of the guidebooks. We may attempt to intervene by including ourselves or our companions in the frame with an object of pilgrimage; but we succeed only in ratifying the power of the monument. We may seek to appropriate the object to our own personal vision: in practice we appear merely as adjuncts to the object, illustrations of its magical power to draw reverential or irreverent attention. Our attempts at authentic personal experience become incorporated into a powerful, quasi-religious ideology.

In a riverside park at Stratford stands a statuary group: in the centre a large pedestal surmounted by the figure of Shakespeare, sitting like patience on a monument, smiling at the bus station. He is surrounded on four sides by the creatures of his imagination: Lady Macbeth, Falstaff, Prince Hal, and of course Hamlet, staring philosophically at the obligatory skull. The iconic emblem of Hamlet holding the skull is the most universal Shakespearean image: frequently confused with the 'To be or not to be' soliloquy, it stands for the transcendent wisdom of the prince of poets. The great contemplative genius gazes stoically, with meditative calm and philosophical resignation, through the mysteries of life and death. Here the bronze statue of the prince is coated with green verdigris; but not so the skull. The corruption of time which ought more properly to encrust the dead than the living form, is absent from the skull: effaced by the reverential touching of generations of pilgrims.

~&

The touristic component of the Shakespeare industry has a history coterminous with the origins of the plays themselves. Much of the most significant evidence in existence about the Elizabethan and Jacobean theatres originates from the recorded observations of travellers. The only visual documentary record of an early Elizabethan public playhouse is the familiar sketch made by the Dutchman, Johannes de Witt. The recorded observations of tourists provide much more information about the theatres than any home-grown, native evidence: the Germans Samuel Kiechel, Thomas Platter, Paul Henzner; the wide-eyed Venetian Busino, who visited the Fortune in 1617; the French ambassador who took his wife to the Globe to see *Pericles* in 1607; the Spanish ambassador who went to the Fortune in 1621, and afterwards banqueted with the players; and a stream of titled dignitaries who patronised the playhouses, such as Prince Lewis Frederick of Württemberg, Prince Otto of Hesse-Cassel, Prince Lewis of Anhalt-Cöthen and Duke Philip Julius of Stettin-Pomerania.[21] Normally these eye-witness accounts have been used as objective documents of theatre history but it is useful also to look *at* as well as *through* them, and consider the inbuilt distortions necessarily endemic to such testimonies.

There is more foreign than domestic evidence for simple reasons: foreign travellers noted what they saw because they found it remarkable; they recorded what they saw because they were educated, literate observers of an only partially literate culture and because, as travellers, they were keeping diaries and writing letters and despatches to their families or employers back home. Native observers could not be expected to share this shock of confronting the striking and original; many, being illiterate, could hardly have written it down if they had. Many lettered native observers were prejudiced on moral or religious grounds against the theatre and so produced accounts with an opposite bias to that of the enthralled foreign tourists. For the manifest disparity between foreign and native accounts lies in the preponderance among visiting observers of extravagant praise, rapturous wonder and enthralled excitement. Such native sources as there are differ remarkably in their strikingly phlegmatic matter-of-factness. John Stow's *Survey of London* mentions the existence of theatres in the city with deadpan impassivity: 'Of late time ... hath been used comedies, tragedies, interludes, and histories, both true and feigned; for the acting whereof certain public places as the Theatre, the Curteine etc. have been created'.[22] Fynes Moryson in his *Itinerary* seems to wonder what all the fuss was about: he refers to certain 'peculiar theatres', drawing 'strange concourse of people', the latter 'being naturally more newe-fangled than the Athenians to heare newes and gaze upon every toye'.[23] It would be interesting to speculate to what extent the rapturous wonder of foreign tourists fuelled the characteristic rhetoric which later retrospectively reconstructed the Elizabethan 'Golden Age'.

It is very probable that the surviving evidence for the presence of foreign tourists within the audiences of Elizabethan public playhouses reflects a disproportionate emphasis, and that in practice they were numerically insignificant. It seems very likely that theatrical entrepreneurs would do what they could to inveigle foreign travellers to the theatres for the plays often, of course, contained matters of international interest and satirical portraits of other nationalities. But the early public playhouses presumably drew for their clientele primarily on a local metropolitan audience. Nonetheless, an important consequence of the establishing from the 1570s of a centralised metropolitan theatrical profession occupying purpose-built theatres in or around London, was the provision of a specific cultural venue to which tourists might be drawn. As the theatre became incorporated, notwithstanding complex and pervasive conflicts of interest, into the new political and cultural hegemony of the metropolis, so the drama became a prestigious possession of the new national state. As Thomas Heywood testified: 'Playing is an ornament to the city, which strangers of all nations, repairing hither, report of in their countries, beholding them here with some admiration: for what variety of entertainment can there be in any city of Christendom, more than in London?'[24] The economic dependence of the RSC, at Stratford and the Barbican, on international tourism, began there: far from being victims of such commercial exploitation, Shakespeare's plays helped to bring it into being. Shakespeare belonged to a new class fraction of bourgeois entrepreneurs which shaped the drama as a privately owned and state-subsidised cultural industry, and decisively effected the radical separation of theatre from the general texture of social life.[25] That class helped to establish a cultural pattern in which every spectator is encouraged to become a tourist: who may well undertake a lengthy journey to a metropolitan theatre, who is required to attend at the dramatic event with reverence and possibly some incomprehension – and who returns with a souvenir programme as a mnemonic preservation of a sacred experience.

⁓

This is the spiritual heart of the Shakespeare myths: and the institutions of bardolatry and quasi-religious worship are the structures holding that myth in place. Myth is not a non-existent fantasy or ideological conjuring trick: it is a real and powerful form of human consciousness, holding some significant place within a culture. It is not possible to banish such a myth by appealing to provable facts, such as those of Shakespeare's biography, or the texts of the plays themselves. The myth itself also has to be subjected to analysis, its ideological content disclosed and its hegemonic position challenged by the invoking of alternative perspectives.

It is often believed that only primitive societies have myths but the figure of Shakespeare is actually very similar to the 'culture heroes' of anthropology: figures which may be legendary heroes, fabulised historical characters or mythological deities but which exhibit, throughout the countless mythologies of world culture, certain common structural characteristics. Consider, for example, the legend which arose in the eighteenth century about Shakespeare's youthful poaching of deer in Sir Thomas Lucy's park: a crime which reputedly resulted in his fleeing to London. Those scholars who demonstrated that Sir Thomas Lucy had at the time neither park nor deer were missing the point: the historical details were merely narrative properties necessary for mythologising Shakespeare as a culture-hero, exhibiting the characteristic pattern of a misspent youth, and the confrontation with a persecutor who thrusts the youth into exile. But the most relevant structural pattern here is a problem of identity: a mystery about the hero's true parentage – he is never the person he appears to be. Folklore, fairy tales and romances abound in figures who are brought up by peasants, shepherds, servants but whose true parents are kings and queens, aristocrats or gods. Who was Robin Hood – son of a Saxon yeoman, or of Robert, Earl of Huntingdon? Who was William Shakespeare – Francis Bacon or the Earl of Oxford? Son of a provincial glover or a scion of the aristocracy or *haute bourgeoisie*?[26]

Ultimately it is this myth that explains the old quarrels about the true authorship of Shakespeare's plays. Shakespeare was the son of a Stratford small businessman but England's greatest poet must surely have had a more exalted parentage. So he became Lord Bacon, the Earl of Oxford, Sir Walter Raleigh, Queen Elizabeth herself. These controversies still rumble on in the peripheries of the scholarly word but the basic *mythos* recently surfaced at one of the centres of Shakespeare scholarship and criticism. The old myth-makers used to employ arcane cabbalistic ciphers to locate the initials of Bacon among Shakespeare's writings; the modern mythologist comes armed with the more formidable tools of computer programmes and statistical analysis.

In November 1985 Gary Taylor, joint editor with Stanley Wells of the prestigious *Oxford Shakespeare*, offered to the public interest a supposedly 'lost Shakespearean love poem': an untitled lyric discovered in a seventeenth-century anthology and now familiarly known by its opening words, 'Shall I die?' The poem is attributed to Shakespeare in the anthology, and Taylor believes the ascription to be reliable. Furthermore, he subjected the poem to computerised tests of vocabulary and syntax, which seemed to him conclusive proof of authorship. This 'discovery' was fed to the press and fêted with substantial media 'hype', and headlines of the 'How Gary discovered the Bard's lost poem' variety.[27] A battle of wits then ensued between those who agreed that Taylor was correct and those who did not. The terms of the debate were scholarly: is the manuscript ascription to Shakespeare reliable and are the language checks trustworthy? – and critical: is the poem good enough to have been written by Shakespeare? The methods of scholarship were both defended and denounced, and the general critical opinion has been that the poem is so 'bad' that it must either have been written by someone else or by Shakespeare in a spirit of parody.[28] As the wrath of the literary-critical establishment, incensed at the attribution to the Bard of a bad and boring poem, fell on him, Gary Taylor began to appear in the progressive light of a scholar displacing the grounds of textual enquiry from bardolatry to scientific method.

The whole debate has, however, been framed by the Shakespeare myth, because it has centred on only one question: did Shakespeare write the poem or not? The poem may or may not have been written by William Shakespeare but a preoccupation with the validating qualities of authorial authority leads to the wrong questions being asked. If we were to approach the poem in terms of its genre and cultural function rather than with a hypothesis of individual authorship, it would be possible both to raise and answer a different set of questions: concerning the formulaic rather than individualistic methods of composing lyric poetry in the Renaissance, the dependence of certain kinds of poetry on the context of musical setting, the intertextuality of a poem's position within a personal manuscript anthology, and so forth.[29] In the kind of debate precipitated by 'Shall I die?', the myth of Shakespeare as a culture hero, as transcendent genius and omniscient seer, is continually reaffirmed.

The true content of that myth, which can be decoded from a long history of intellectual struggle around the problem of identity, is that the concept of individual authorship on which most Shakespeare criticism is based is a misleading way of addressing the work of an Elizabethan/Jacobean dramatist; perhaps, following Foucault, a mythical concept in itself.[30] The theoretical problematic is analogous to the cultural pattern of the tourist industry: everything in Stratford must be definitively assigned to the personal possession of the Bard or it becomes

worthless and irrelevant. The theatre must be 'Shakespeare's' theatre, an exhibition of Elizabethan England must be 'The World of
Shakespeare' and signs directing the traveller to 'The Birthplace'
betray, by their striking anonymity, the monopolistic character of
Shakespeare's authorship of Stratford.

Those scholars who speculated that Shakespeare might perhaps have been somebody else, or a group of authors, were asking
the wrong questions but they were at least grappling with a genuine problem. We cannot rely, when addressing the work of a
Renaissance dramatist, on the apparent clarity and simplicity of a
direct, controlling relationship between author and written text.
These plays were made and mediated in the interaction of certain
complex material conditions, of which the author was only one.
When we deconstruct the Shakespeare myth what we discover is
not a universal individual genius creating literary texts that
remain a permanently valuable repository of human experience
and wisdom; but a collaborative cultural process in which plays
were made by writers, theatrical entrepreneurs, architects and
craftsmen, actors and audience – a process in which the plays
were constructed first as performance, and only subsequently
given the formal permanence of print. As Terry Hawkes observes:

> The notion of a single "authoritative" text, immediately expressive
> of the plenitude of its author's mind and meaning, would have
> been unfamiliar to Shakespeare, involved as he was in the collabo-
> rative enterprise of dramatic production, and notoriously uncon-
> cerned to preserve in stable form the texts of most of his plays. A
> project which seeks to award those texts the status of holy writ …
> [is] the product of a culture which characteristically invests a
> good deal of intellectual capital in concepts of individuality, per-
> sonal ownership and responsibility, and maintains a high regard
> for the printed text as a personal unmediated statement, particu-
> larly in the form of "literature".[31]

Stratford genuinely can, then, as F.J. Furnivall suggested in the quotation that heads this essay, help us to understand Shakespeare – though in a sense rather different from that he and many others have traditionally intended.

CHAPTER EIGHT

Shakesperean Features (1991)

(WITH BRYAN LOUGHREY)

O sweet Mr Shakespeare, Ile have his picture in my study[1]

L IKE MANY ARTISTS, W.B. Yeats conceived of the relation between life and art in terms of an aesthetic of Platonic ideal ism. The poet, he declared, is never the bundle of accidents and incoherences that sits down to breakfast; he has been reborn as an idea, something intended, complete.[2] This disembodied authorial presence inhabiting the text rather than the world is, of course, a commonplace of literary criticism. George Orwell, for example, concludes his essay 'Charles Dickens' with this extraordinary fantastia:

> When one reads any strongly individual piece of writing, one has the impression of seeing a face somewhere behind the page. I feel this very strongly with Swift, with Defoe, with Fielding, Stendhal, Thackeray, Flaubert, though in several cases I do not know what these people looked like and do not want to know. What one sees is the face the writer ought to have. Well, in the case of Dickens I see a face that is not quite the face of Dickens's photographs, although it resembles it. It is the face of a man about forty, with a small beard and a high colour. He is laughing, with a touch of anger in his laughter, but no triumph, no malignity. It is the face of a man who is generously angry – in other words, of a nineteenth-century liberal, a free intelligence, a type hated by all the smelly little orthodoxies which are now contending for our souls.[3]

Physiognomy and literary criticism here coalesce. Dickens's fiction is read in the light of a powerfully realised image of its author. This image is, however, perceived as an idealised construct, 'the face that the writer *ought* to have', dependent upon a particular interpretation of the literary evidence. The critic's X-ray vision penetrates the patina of the text to reveal the author's true presence 'behind the page'. Or so Orwell would have us believe.

But it can surely be no accident that the idealised portrait of the novelist (which, of course, is also an unconscious self-portrait) which the critic finds, turns out to resemble so closely the face to be seen in surviving photographs of Dickens. Orwell's disclaimers (his lack of interest in what authors *actually* looked like and the merely grudging acknowledgement of the fact that his idealised Dickens is modelled on an image ultimately derived from real flesh and blood) betray a nervous embarrassment with the intertextual procedure adopted – one can almost hear Jonson's injunction echoing down the centuries, 'Reader, looke/Not on his Picture, but his Book'![4] But it is in fact two very real texts, one literary and one photographic, which are read in conjunction to construct Orwell's Dickens. Word and image prove mutually dependent, each validating a precarious critical judgement founded in part on both.

Orwell's embarrassment, however, is misplaced. For one thing, he is in good company. His procedure is one that has been often adopted, albeit in a more guarded fashion, by professional critics of the academic establishment. Here, for example, is Anne Barton on Ben Jonson: 'In the famous, and much copied, portrait of the mature Jonson attributed to Abraham van Blyenberch, the sitter almost seems to belong to a different race from Sidney, Spenser, Marlow, Raleigh and Donne – or even from Shakespeare who stares out from the woodenly inept Droeshout engraving. Jonson's broad, blunt, vigorously plain face dissociates itself oddly in any portrait gallery from the more elegant, attenuated faces of his Elizabethan contemporaries. His artistic detachment from them, during much of his life, was equally radical.'[5] Here a substantive critical evaluation is located, rhetorically if not in logic, in the physiognomic differences offered by contemporary portraiture. The intertextuality of word and image is harnessed to the purposes of a characterising and distinguishing literary judgement of the artist's work.

The critical practice of both Orwell and Barton points towards issues of considerable theoretical significance. Literary works are not, after all, Platonic ideas, but exist in material culture. They have no life outside of the contexts in which they are read. And the meanings which they generate in and for any given culture are determined cumulatively by a wide range of factors which include 'how they are edited, what kinds of commentary they generate, whether they are translated into other languages, how often they are quoted, how they (and their author's name) are spelled, *how they (and their author) are visually represented*' (our italics).[6] This essay focuses on a few of those images of Shakespeare which have helped shape the way we read his works, and attempts to destabilise the traditional hierarchy of discourses in which hermeneutic appropriations of dramatic literature and poetic language rank far higher than the material processes through which poetry and drama circulate within a culture.

Shakespeare's face is one of the most insistently reproduced icons in the world. It adorns countless book covers, hotel and restaurant signs, beer mats, tea caddies, confectionery packets, cigarette and playing cards, ceramics, theatre and museum foyers, advertisements, and banknotes. Its currency is based in large measure on the cachet of high culture (Shakespeare metaphorically authorises those products he vicariously and posthumously endorses), combined with its instant recognisability. The high balding dome – 'what a forehead, what a brain!'[7] – has been parodied by Picasso and innumerable other artists and become an almost totemic guarantor of the author's unique genius. In that iconic image we can read a discourse both acculturated and commodified, constituted by the alien but strategically related languages of art and economics, bardolatry and business. From its accrued historical traces, and from the cultural and economic contexts in which it has been mobilised, we can decode from this image the embodiment of a symbol: a symbol, pre-eminently, of British national culture. It is this symbolic 'Shakespeare' we encounter as an image that permeates the fabric and texture of everyday common life. It is probable that every English-speaking citizen of the UK is acquainted with Shakespeare; not necessarily from plays and books, but from the visual images borne by the ubiquitous advertisements, tourist attractions, pub signs, biscuit tins, credit cards and calendars. An agency offering elocution lessons used to advertise itself through a cartoon drawing of a puzzled Shakespeare, bewildered by a voice from a telephone receiver: to be understood by 'Shakespeare' would be a guarantee of correct speech. In the television series *Batman*, the entrance to the 'Batcave' is controlled by a switch concealed within a bust of Shakespeare: the decorative property of a millionaire's house opens to activate an exotic world of drama and costume, fantasy and adventure. The *Radio Times* once carried a cover design, heralding a programme on language, the 'Story of English' ('the great adventure which transformed the island speech of Shakespeare into the world English of 1,000 million'), entitled 'From Will to the World' in which the imperial, brain-impacted forehead of the Bard, set amidst an English pastoral landscape, had swelled to encompass 'the great globe itself'.

❧

But from whence do we derive this familiar received image of the

'The Droeshout Engraving', taken from the first folio.
Reproduced by kind permission of the British Library ▷

Mr. William
SHAKESPEARES

COMEDIES,
HISTORIES, &
TRAGEDIES.

Published according to the True Originall Copies.

Martin Droeshout sculpsit London.

national poet? There are only two portraits of Shakespeare which have claims to 'Authenticity', Gheerhart Janssen's bust in Holy Trinity Church, Stratford, and Martin Droeshout's title-page engraving to the 1623 First Folio. Both were commissioned some years after Shakespeare's death and probably both relied on some form of preliminary sketch supplied by friends or relatives. They seem to have been acceptable to those who commissioned them, although this in no way guarantees any certainty of realism on the part of the artists. Although they depict what is obviously the same man, there are striking differences between them in their modes of representation. The Janssen bust honours the well-to-do Stratford burgher, offering us a corpulent, older man with up-turned, trimmed moustaches, neatly bobbed side-locks, expensively tailored robes, who holds in his hands the stylised reminders of the source of his wealth in the foregrounded pen and sheet of paper.

The image of the Droeshout Shakespeare, with its younger, more dishevelled appearance and encephalous forehead, has proved, despite the seventeen year-old engraver's obvious technical incompetence in such matters as relating the proportion of the head to that of the torso, the more popular image of the artist. Some scholars have therefore felt free to hijack Shakespeare's features and mould them to something more approximating the Shakespeare of their own conception. Edmund Malone attempted the most extreme form of revisionism on record. In 1793, in search of a neo-classical paradigm, he persuaded the vicar of Holy Trinity to have the original gaudy paintwork of the Janssen bust whitewashed, earning the opprobrium of a contemporary pilgrim who, acutely noting the conjunction of aesthetic and editorial vandalism, adapted for his own anathematisation the curse engraved on Shakespeare's tombstone:

> Stranger, to whom this monument is shewn
> Invoke the Poet's curse upon Malone;
> Whose meddling zeal his barbarous taste betrays,
> And daubs his tombstones, as he mars his plays![8]

But generally critics have confined themselves to championing one or other of the various rival portraits.[9] Scholars have detected in the aesthetic and semiotic differences between portraits appropriate impressions of the Bard's personality: romantic bravura in the Chandos, sensitive aristocratic features in the Janssen, a gentle, pensive expression in the Felton, and a soulful gaze in the Grafton. All these are, predictably, the qualities these same scholars admire and want to find in their matchless Bard. Samuel Schoenbaum is surely right to suggest that, whatever else they are, these portraits are an index of the way our greatest poet has been imagined, functioning as Rorschach blots onto which the critic 'projects the image of his own conceit'.[10]

ᴥ

Caroline Spurgeon, for example, wanted to use the so-called 'Chess Portrait'[11] of Shakespeare and Jonson as the cover illustration for her *Shakespeare's Imagery*:

> No other presentation I have yet seen of Shakespeare approaches it in satisfying quality. You will find in the face thought, imagination, great intellectual power, great sensitiveness and refinement, and altogether a feeling of strength and power behind sensitiveness which is remarkable.[12]

What is most remarkable, of course, is that these are precisely the qualities she detected in Shakespeare's imagery. Disarmingly, Spurgeon admits to the charge of wish-fulfilment: 'If there is one thing certain in a world of uncertainties, it is that Shakespeare did not look like the Droeshout portrait. On the other hand he might have looked like the man to the right in the 'chess portrait'; so, for my part, I prefer to look at that.'[13]

There were, of course, financial imperatives to many of the visual appropriations. The explosion of demand for Shakespeariana which began in the eighteenth century led to the 'discovery' of a host of 'Shakespeare' portraits. Some were perfectly genuine early paintings of individuals whose features happened to include a high forehead (and therefore 'must' be of Shakespeare).[14] But many were the productions of such enterprising forgers as the celebrated Paul Zincke, who carefully reworked old canvasses and then artificially aged the overpainting. Such counterfeits were so common in the nineteenth century that Lionel Cust, Director of the National Portrait Gallery, reckoned on being offered more than one a year, usually at an extravagant price. Some of the better counterfeits, such as the Folger Library's famous Ashbourne portrait, have only recently been exposed as fakes.[15] More insidiously, the enormous sums of money which a genuine portrait could command tended to cloud scholarly judgement. The owner of the 'chess portrait', for example, sent it for verification to Paul Wislicenus, the author of several books on the so-called 'Kesselstadt Death Mask'. Perhaps it should not be particularly surprising to find that, on very flimsy evidence, Wislicenus came to a firm conviction of the portrait's authenticity, bearing in mind the fact that the contract he negotiated with the painting's owner guaranteed him ten per cent of the eventual sale price of the portrait.[16]

Commercial considerations have, of course, always surrounded Shakespearean portraiture. The Droeshout engraving, for example, owes its origins to enterprising literary entrepreneurs and a new conception of the nature of authorship. It is probable that Shakespeare subscribed to the then common view which sharply distinguished between works of literature and play-texts. Plays were generally regarded as light entertainment, the property of the theatrical houses that commissioned them, often from a pool of anonymous hacks. Shakespeare went to his grave without ever having seen plays of the stature of *Macbeth, Antony and Cleopatra,* or *The Tempest* reach print. Those plays that had been published had appeared in cheap quarto format with few signs of authorial supervision. It is therefore tempting to agree with Terence Hawkes that 'The notion of a single "authoritative" text, immediately expressive of the plenitude of its author's mind and meaning, would have been unfamiliar to Shakespeare, involved as he was in the collaborative enterprise of dramatic production, and notoriously unconcerned to preserve in stable form the texts of most of his plays.'[17]

⁑

Hawkes's view, however, needs to be treated with care. It applies specifically to Shakespeare's dramatic output and it appears that he regarded his 'literary' output in a very different light. Both *Venus and Adonis* and *The Rape of Lucrece* were published in carefully prepared copy, complete with signed dedicatory epistles to the Earl of Southampton, with evidence of careful authorial supervision. Within Shakespeare's lifetime, moreover, Ben Jonson had already staked a claim for a far loftier status for the true playwright, who was a poet rather than the follower of the 'trade of the stage, in all their mis'line enterludes'.[18] In the year of Shakespeare's death he brought out the first-ever collected edition of English dramatic texts, *The Workes of Beniamin Jonson*, a carefully prepared and expensively produced folio volume, featuring an engraved title-page, Latin epigrams, epistles dedicatory and the Vaughan portrait of the poet (the only one which can be proved to have been executed during his lifetime).[19] It bore, in fact, the hallmark of a prestige publication, although its contents included not only his incidental poetry and court masques, but also a selection of those plays he had written for the public and private theatres, even going to the length of including the cast lists of the original productions. The text of *Sejanus*, a play originally written with an unknown collaborator, was carefully revised to preserve the purity of authorial input.

Jonson's 'presumption' did not go unnoticed and provoked derisive comment: 'Pray tell me, Ben,' a wit demanded,

> where doth the mystery lurk,
> What others call a play, you call a work.[20]

Jonson's *Works* were nonetheless commercially successful and probably inspired William Jaggard and Thomas Pavier to initiate the publication of Shakespeare's plays in a multi-volume edition. They were restrained from completing this venture by the Lord Chamberlain, probably after complaint from the King's Men. Jaggard and his son Isaac, however, went on to print the First Folio, MR. WILLIAM SHAKESPEARE'S COMEDIES, HISTORIES, & TRAGEDIES. Like Jonson's *Works* this was an expensively produced volume, which probably accounts for the fact that the publication was a risky venture undertaken by a consortium of stationers. The 1,200 or so volumes printed sold at the premium price of £1 and came adorned with a full panoply of dedications and commendatory verses, as well as the Droeshout engraving. What it is important to recognise is that the general tendency of these introductory materials is to personalise the plays, to attach them firmly to the author rather than to the theatrical milieu in which they had been first produced. The early quartos of his plays had tended to stress theatrical rather than authorial provenance. The title page of the popular *Titus Andronicus*, for example, merely records that it was 'Plaide by the Right Honourable the Earle of Darbie, Earle of Pembrooke, and Earle of Sussex their Servants', and not until 1598 was Shakespeare's name attached to a printed version of one of his plays, *Love's Labour's Lost*. Heminge and Condel instead emphasise Shakespeare's 'authorly' status and the 'readerly', literary nature of the texts, 'reade him, therefore; and againe and againe'[21] (they were well aware also of the commercial dimension of the project: 'read, and censure. Do so, but buy it first.'). Similarly, in their commendatory verses, Jonson focuses on 'my beloved, The Author', Hugh Holland on the 'Scenicke Poet', Leonard Digges, 'the deceased Author' and I.M. simply 'the memorie of M.W. Shakespeare'.

The Droeshout engraving, strategically placed on the title-page, has to be viewed in this context, a personalising, validating presence, literally authorising the works that follow. Ben Jonson's accompanying epigram, 'To the Reader', is less obviously part of this strategy, but plays its role. At first glance it seems to direct attention away from the image of the author towards the works themselves, 'Reader, looke/Not on his Picture, but his Booke'. But, of course, it is impossible to obey this injunction. Jonson's lines appear on the verso but Shakespeare's face dominates the recto; neither can be viewed without sight of the other. Engraving and epigram prove mutually dependent, constituting a unified design, the effect of which is to invite 'the Reader' to view the plays in the context of a formidable authorial presence. Early purchasers of the First Folio, that is, were at the beginning of a process with which all modern readers of Shakespeare must be familiar, coming to the plays having first confronted a carefully constructed picture of a culture hero, transcendent genius and omniscient seer. In an important article on new bibliographical approaches, Roger Chartier provides a theoretical foundation for the point:

> 'Forms effect meaning' ... To attend to the material, formal inscriptions of literary works goes against that spontaneous and misleading image which readers have of their relation to a text as being a transparent and purely intellectual one. It reminds us of the unsuspected power of signs whose supposed insignificance generally leads us to overlook them, such as (to speak only of the printed book) the format chosen, the division and layout of the text on the page, the place of illustrations, the organisation of reference and notes, and so on.'[22]

One of the most familiar representations of Shakespeare derives from a key moment of historical transition in this strange eventful history, that point where the face of Shakespeare, shadowy and inscrutable in darkening canvases, was actualised into the relative fixity and permanence of statuary form, seeking and finding a marble or a bronze repose. The creation of a sculpted bust or statue is, of course, a different process of artistic production, implying different social relationships and different cultural purposes. The first sculpture of Shakespeare was the funereal effigy in Holy Trinity church at Stratford, where the formal properties of the representation are at one level a contribution to the surrounding ecclesiastical architecture. Despite the self-evident spirituality of the context, and the artistic bravura of the ostentatiously flourished quill pen, this particular image has not provided Shakespeare's admirers with an acceptable effigy, a suitable objective correlative for the amazing monument of his artistic achievement. In his own funereal bust Shakespeare looked, to John Dover Wilson, like a 'self-satisfied pork-butcher'.[23] If one knew no better, the pen wielded by this portly Stratford bourgeois could just as well be recording a retailer's business transactions as forming the dramatic poetry of *King Lear*, penning (in Keats's words) 'red-lined accounts' rather than 'the songs of Grecian years'.

Shakespeare was not after all entitled to a burial space in the chancel of Stratford church on account of his poetic or theatrical achievement but because he was a local landholder and lessee of tithes. If the image depicted by this bust forms the characteristic features of a complacent Stratford bourgeois, then there is no reason in principle why they should not have been assigned to Shakespeare, son of a local tradesman, successful professional and businessman, shrewd investor and property speculator. In Dover Wilson's complaint can be heard the accent of that aristocratic revulsion from the bourgeois origins of the national bard, which is the basis of so many claims, on Shakespeare's behalf, for an alternative and superior social identity.

The visual languages used to represent persons were in this period only partly concerned with accurate physical representation. The discourses of portraiture were also designed to represent, through the development of visual conventions, general categories of social type, historical contexts, ideas and values. The question of whether Shakespeare at the point of death actually looked like the bust in Holy Trinity church is perhaps more an anachronistic curiosity of the modern photographic imagination than a proper concern of the seventeenth-century plastic artist, who was probably more interested in the question of whether the image 'looked like' whatever the individual's family and friends, the commissioners of the portrait, the commercial and professional middle class of Stratford and the governors of the church wanted to signify by means of the statue.

sa

Sculpture from this period tends to commemorate rather than imitate the person, overtly using the person's physical attributes as a source for the direct communication of cultural meaning. The best-known sculpted representation of Shakespeare, source of many stone and metal imitations, is the marble statue commissioned by public subscription, executed by Peter Scheemakers and erected in Westminster Abbey as a memorial to the national poet in 1741. It functioned therefore both as a collective tribute, drawing on what was already a substantial fund of reverence and admiration; a memorialisation of a pre-eminent genius of English culture and an official emblematisation of Shakespeare's reception into the structures of national authority and power, constituted by church, state and monarchy. Housed in Westminster Abbey, the image of a writer becomes expressive of the spirit of a nation. Here representation is at its most impersonal, a lapidary codification of the signs of cultural power. The features of Shakespeare scarcely resemble any of the earlier portraits, but are constituted by those conventions of idealised depiction which transformed the eighteenth-century English aristocracy into a pantheon of classical characters. Within an impersonal and idealising texture provided by the cold chastity of the medium, this figure etches the faces into the sharp, clean lines of an 'English' countenance. A clear, candid spirituality further hints (especially in the shaping of the hair and beard) at a similarity to the icon of Christ.[24]

The semiotics of the statue also enact in microcosm a relation between the figure and its institutional space. The form of Shakespeare is shown leaning on a pedestal, embossed with the faces of a pantheon of English monarchs. The supportive pedestal expresses monumental authority and links the image to its surrounding context of royal and state power. The figure by contrast expresses relaxed contemplation and nonchalant mastery; the pose is derived from the conventional Elizabethan image of the melancholy young man leaning against a tree (as in Nicholas Hillyard's miniature). Thus the artefact juxtaposes the weight and stability of the monumental context against an aristocratic insouciance, a relaxed grace and elegant langour appropriate to the eighteenth-century image of the man-of-letters. The pile of books surmounting the pedestal partakes of both dimensions: the solid, weighty, heavily bound records of monumental achievement, they are merely a prop for the casual elbow of the leaning poet, rapt in an impassioned stillness of meditation.

Like a Coronation mug, this particular icon offered the perfect form for reproduction and circulation, and as a miniature souvenir became a standard item in the old curiosity shops of Stratford-upon-Avon. The history of its reproduction actually began very early, and in a context that neatly illustrates the relationship between bardolatrous reverence for the symbol of cultural hegemony, and its reduction to tourist curiosity in the acquisition of commodified bardic mementos. In the form of a leaden copy executed in a mass production factory at Hyde Park corner, Scheemakers' statue appeared as a centre-piece in David Garrick's Great Shakespeare Jubilee, held in Stratford in 1769. This event, which was at one level a genuine tribute to Shakespeare from a great man of theatre, was also the ancestor of all the rituals of organised silliness that have since occurred, and are still occurring, around the name, fame and reputation of Shakespeare.

Garrick's celebration, which really put the tiny West Midlands market town of Stratford on the map, was as much about Garrick as it was about Shakespeare: a contemporary illustration shows the actor-manager declaiming his great bardolatrous Ode, with the statue well in the background (the best place to be, considering some of the lines Garrick was delivering):

> Untouched and sacred be thy shrine
> Avonian Willy! Bard Divine!

Garrick's Jubilee can be regarded as the great formal inauguration of bardolatry as a national religion; the moment, in the words of one scholar, which 'marks the point at which Shakespeare stopped being regarded as an increasingly popular and admirable dramatist, and became a god'.[25] At the same time, it employed as a central symbolic icon an image of Shakespeare which became, in a later age of mechanical reproduction, an instantly recognisable souvenir. The movement from fetished object of worship to fetished token of commodity production is a graphic curve typical of the cultural distribution of the Shakespeare industry.

٭

The contradictory apotheosis of this statuesque image is its incorporation into the design of the British £20 note, where the mystical aura of monumental magnificence and the millionfold multiplicity of mechanical reproduction occupy a single dimension. The device on the banknote transacts a complex exchange of values: the currency of Shakespeare as a cultural token, a symbol both of high art and national pride, enhances the material worth of the promissory note; while the high value of the note itself confers a corresponding richness on the symbol of national culture. A bank note is both a sign of value and a legal contract, a 'bond' between citizen and state: the exchange of such symbolic tokens represents both a constitutive material activity and a process of bonding and socialisation. The fortunate holder of a

Shakespeareanised banknote possesses both monetary wealth and aesthetic richness; and by virtue of that possession is integrated, both materially and culturally, into the dominant ideology of a monetarist society. Here the solid bulk of another major apparatus of British society, the Bank of England, is articulated with the marble gravity of Shakespeare and the immense solidity of Westminster Abbey, in an institutional configuration grouped to link the strength of a currency with the power of traditional authority.

The paper portrait of Shakespeare probably represents the culmination of eighteenth-century bardolatry – but it represents also its terminal point. Here all the contradictions of the bardic ideology are held in a paradoxical unity. That which is specific, unique, supremely individual, here appears in its most generalised, impersonal form. The incomparable, irreplaceable, unrepeatable genius of Shakespeare is fragmented by the process of mechanical reproduction into millions of identical simulacra. Those specialised public domains which are in reality the private spaces of our society's prominent individuals, are here offered for imaginative occupation by anyone possessed of that minimal financial qualification, as Buckingham Palace used to be occupied every morning by a million breakfast plates slapped onto a million cheap table-mats. But the overriding premise of this ideological structure is that authority and power are vested in the material presence of a concrete substance, embodied in the solidity and weight of a positivistic 'reality'. The banknote may be merely fragile paper, but it bears the signature of authority, the images of reliability, the stamp of power. The mysterious potency symbolised by the financial token is by definition absent (even a banknote is really abstract 'credit' for it declares itself explicitly to be a 'promise') but it is a god with a countenance of marble, with feet of lead and with printing presses of solid steel. What happens however when, as we see today, the identity of money as abstract value supersedes and obliterates the character of money as material substance?

৵

In the contemporary social economy money is debt and credit, profit and investment, the cheque and the credit card, figures scrolling across a computer screen or printed on a bank statement, as much for the private citizen as for the industrialist or commercial entrepreneur. Wealth is no longer piled up in greasy banknotes, or accumulated amid the clashing cacophony of industrial production, but amassed through the technological media of computers and carphones, realised in the vaccuous non-existence of the futures market. Commercial exchange at even the simplest level is as likely to proceed via the paper or plastic authorisation of credit, as through an exchange of physical tokens like coins or notes. Clearly, if the traditional resources of culture are to be mobilised in support of these developments, they will require new forms of representation. Enter the 'Bard-card'.

The traditional iconography of Shakespeare reproduction traded in effects of mass and solidity, gravity and substance. We now witness the evolution of a new 'post-modern' iconography, appropriate to a society where money can be referred to as 'plastic'. Like the £20 note, cheque guarantee cards issued by some banks carry a picture of Shakespeare. Where on the banknote the bardic image only symbolically authorised value, on the Bardcard it does so literally, since the image is depicted in the form of a high technology visual 'hologram', designed to inhibit fraudulent use and reproduction. The hologram was developed from a photograph, which is not (as one might reasonably expect) a copy of one of the standard Shakespeare portraits, but a photo of a costumed actor pretending to look like Shakespeare.

The authenticity of the card is thus demonstrated not by a display of cultural power but by a technological coup d'oeil. In terms of content, the image approaches grotesque self-parody, since the proof of individual ownership, by the cardholder, of certain resources of credit held by a bank, is attested by the most fraudulent and artificial means imaginable: a hologram of a photograph of an actor pretending to be ... Shakespeare. Where the traditional imagery of the Scheemakers statue invoked cultural and economic solidity, the image of the Bardcard is pure post-modernist surface, yielding to the efforts of interpretation only a ludicrous self-reflexive playfulness. Where the £20 note points to the legitimate state ownership and control of both economic and cultural power, the Bardcard proves your title to credit by display-ing the image of a major author whose responsibility for the cul-tural productions attributed to him has been consistently and systematically questioned. This quality is compounded by the reverse of the card, where the holder's signature authorises indi-vidual ownership of its power, irresistibly recalling the illegible scrawl of the six signatures attributed to Shakespeare, which some experts have described as apparently belonging to six differ-ent people, at least three of them illiterate or terminally ill. One wonders how the bank would react to a cardholder who signed his name with the flexible and cavalier approach to spelling also visible in those 'Shakespearean' autographs.

Has the wheel come full circle, or has the whirligig of time brought in its revenges? Our natural propensity, in contemplating relations between past and present, to imagine a chronological decline from reality to image, from substance to shadow, points us towards the latter explanation. On the other hand, as we have demonstrated, the intertextuality of verbal and visual signs from the earliest stages of 'Shakespeare' reconstruction might persuade us to consider continuity as the keynote of this historical process.

We would not wish our argument to be understood as a crude materialism, a cynical assertion that this immense accumulated repository of cultural production is all nothing more than fraud, forgery and fabrication. Neither would we wish to be perceived as academic alternative comedians, facetiously playing in the marginal spaces of history and culture, demystifying a peripheral area that has never been more than tangentially related to the dominant concerns of literary and theatrical criticism. On the contrary, just as there are clear resemblances between the discourse of bardolatry employed in tourism and advertising, and the language of some twentieth-century Shakespeare criticism, there are striking parallels between the playful irresponsibility of deconstructionist criticism, the eclectic pastiche visible in contemporary theatrical production and the depthless luminescent shimmer of the Bardcard's hologram.

We would like to see both the methods advocated and the materials studied here installed closer to the centre of contemporary criticism. As far as 'Shakespeare' is concerned to reverse Ben Jonson's (in any case ambiguous exhortation) we recommend the reader to look with the same kind of attention here, 'on his Picture', as he or she has been accustomed to exercise in the scrutiny of 'his Booke'.

CHAPTER NINE

Everybody's Shakespeare (1994)

1994 can now rank with 1769 as the year of another 'Great Shake-speare Jubilee', indeed as the year that witnessed 'the first event of its kind in this country and probably the world: an international multi-disciplined celebration of the work and influence of Shake-speare'[1]. This grand Bardfest took the form of a massive two-month Shakespeare extravaganza, mobilised by the Royal Shakespeare Company, and focused on a major theatre season, with an associated series of events and exhibitions at the Barbican Centre. In order that no one should escape this Shakespearean saturation, there was also a wall-to-wall television Shakespeare season, broadcast on BBC2, and entitled 'Bard on the Box'. The latter provided innumerable ten-minute interludes of curious and interesting trivia about Elizabethan culture – from cooking cod-pieces to wearing them – and a number of full length feature programmes on issues such as the development of Shakespeare's reputation as the 'national poet'. One programme, entitled 'The Battle of Wills', addressed the long-running controversy over identity which takes the form of contending claims on the authorship of Shakespeare's plays.

The governing title of the festival was 'Everybody's Shakespeare'.

There is something for everyone, the title suggests, in this broad-ranging and diversified, international and multi-cultural, celebration. Whatever your cultural background and personal preferences, you were bound to find here something of interest. In one sense the title was individualising, speaking to the number and multiplicity of persons. In another sense it was universalising, since the common ground on which this infinitely diversified constituency can meet, the global totality that contains all these individuals, was the one and only 'Shakespeare'. Thus 'Everybody's Shakespeare' was also 'the greatest ever celebration of the genius of Shakespeare'. What enables us collectively to inhabit 'Shakespeare' is not that which particularises and differentiates us, but that which universalises him. This immediate and contemporary availability of Shakespeare can be recognised as yet another manifestation of that universal genius proclaimed by Ben Jonson: 'He was not for an age, but for all time'[2] and still echoed and embodied in the Department for Education's *National Curriculum for English* which sees Shakespeare's plays as so rich that in every age they can produce fresh meanings.[3]

Shakespeare is everybody's. But the syntax allows for another reading: 'Everybody *is* Shakespeare'. This alternative interpretation remains sub-textual in the words but was foregrounded in the festival's publicity leaflet which exhibited a politically correct rent-a-crowd: black, white, yellow; male and female; young and old. Each face peeped cheerfully out from behind the mask of Shakespeare's face in its most familiar representation, the Droeshout engraving from *Mr William Shakespeares Comedies, Histories, & Tragedies* of 1623. Everybody then can become Shakespeare, or at least personify Shakespeare; for the mask is also, of course, the standard symbol of drama, the theatrical prototype for assuming a role, playing a part. We can all play Shakespeare, or play at being Shakespeare, by participation in the proffered ritual of celebration. The Droeshout engraving is particularly appropriate to make this point since (as viewers of the TV programme 'The Battle of Wills' were informed) it has been

Everybody's

Shakespeare

International Festival

suspected, by those concerned to question Shakespeare's true identity, that the face of the portrait is actually a mask. 'No human being could possibly look like that' affirmed one witness, plugging the claims of Christopher Marlowe. Setting aside the improbability of Marlowe's sitting behind a mask while the artist engraved its likeness, we can readily accept that the face *is* notoriously separable from its physical context, since it has become, through continuous familiar usage, an immediately recognisable cultural icon. That which is universal is also anonymous. Why *should* Shakespeare look like any other human being, if he is, by virtue of his 'genius', so essentially *different* from every other human being? 'Looke', Ben Jonson says, 'not on his Picture, but his Booke'.[4] The author had already, by 1623, been subsumed into the work, the 'genius', present in the writing, quite invisible in the face. Anthony Burgess, in the conclusion of his fanciful 'biography' of Shakespeare, plays with this idea and formulates clearly the impossible paradox of genius and universality:[5]

> Martin Droeshout's engraving, ... has never been greatly liked ... The face is that of a commercial traveller growing bald in the service of an ungrateful firm.
>
> We need not repine at the lack of a satisfactory Shakespeare portrait. To see his face, we need only look in a mirror. He is ourselves, ordinary suffering humanity, fired by moderate ambitions, concerned with money, the victim of desire, all too mortal. To his back, like a hump, was strapped a miraculous but somehow irrelevant talent ... We are all Will. Shakespeare is the name of one of our redeemers.

Everybody is Shakespeare, then, minus the hump. Shakespeare is simply one of us, with the hump. The presence or absence of that hump, however, that 'talent' or 'genius', can (we are told) make all

◁ Advertisement for the 'Everybody's Shakespeare International Festival' (1994). *Reproduced by kind permission of the Barbican Centre and the RSC, based on a photograph by Nigel Parry*

the difference between an ordinary mortal and a 'redeemer', a man and a god.

೨ಎ

Shakespeare, the director Michael Bogdanov used to claim, introducing his series of televised workshops *Shakespeare Lives!* 'is the greatest living playwright'.[6] Bogdanov is one of those directors who seek that universality not in timeless abstractions, but in the everyday detail of the contemporary world, amidst the diversity and peculiarity of ordinary lives. His faith is not in an immutable and transhistorical genius, but in the capability of a particular body of writing to be reactivated, mobilised and appropriated in different circumstances and to different ends. Bogdanov's theatrical work with Shakespeare has been criticised on the same grounds as some modern theoretical approaches, including cultural materialism, that in such contemporary appropriations, Shakespeare functions as 'merely the poor sponge that soaks up the various historical, ideological and social discourses of its day'.[7] Yet in some ways, the affirmation that 'Shakespeare Lives!' (the title of Bogdanov's Channel 4 series of televised workshops), that 'Shakespeare is the greatest living playwright', comes very close to Shakespearean universality: not for an age, but for all time. If for all time, then for any time; everybody's Shakespeare, everybody *is* Shakespeare.

But any time, is not all time; and everybody is not Shakespeare. Moreover, Shakespeare is not a living playwright: at one point he was, but now, rest his soul, he's dead. To assign to the dead, either literally or metaphorically, a capability of living speech is to affirm the possibility of transhistorical human continuity, perpetuity of meaning, and unimpeded communication across centuries of historical change. The dead are in this formation, paradoxically, more alive than the living. T.S. Eliot had no doubt that this was literally the case: using the image of the Pentecostal flame, he affirmed in *Little Gidding* that 'the communication / Of the dead is tongued with fire beyond the language of the living'.[8] This is a great truth: yet most of the time the dead have no language other than the speech of the living, even when we are merely repeating the words we have inherited from them.

Stephen Greenblatt, the foremost figure of New Historicism, discusses this problem with great subtlety in *Shakespearean Negotiations*[9]. Greenblatt begins with this paradox: he is an academic, interested in early modern texts, and frequenting them to find out what they mean. At the same time, as a twentieth-century cultural theorist whose views of history, of human nature and of language have been transformed by post-structuralist theory, he believes that there is no transhistorical human nature. History is a contemporary narrative, a story we tell ourselves about the past and language is no transparent and unmediated window onto an objective and independent reality. It is rather, as in post-structuralist theory, a closed system within which all our perceptions and interpretations – including those of history and human nature – are contained. A word or object from the past exists and has meaning only within the system and structure, the perpetual contemporaneity, of living language. When we read a Shakespeare sonnet or observe an Elizabethan building, we are assimilating those objects to our own ideological context and conferring upon them our own modern meanings. But let Greenblatt (mercifully still alive) speak for himself:

> I began with the desire to speak with the dead ... If I never believed that the dead could hear me, and if I knew that the dead could not speak, I was nonetheless certain that I could recreate a conversation with them. Even when I came to understand that in my most intense moments of straining to listen all I could hear was my own voice, even then I could not abandon my desire. It was true that I could hear only my own voice, but my own voice was the voice of the dead, for the dead had contrived to leave textual traces of themselves, and those textual traces make themselves heard in the voice of the living. ... It is paradoxical, of course, to seek the living will of the dead in fictions, in places where there was no live bodily being to begin with. But those who love litera-

ture tend to find more intensity in simulations – in the formal, self conscious miming of life – than in any of the other textual traces left by the dead, for simulations are undertaken in full awareness of the absence of the life they contrive to represent, and hence they may skilfully anticipate and compensate for the vanishing of the actual life that has empowered them (p. 1).

Agnes Heller[10] identified this longing to recover the past as a potent form of 'nostalgia'. Her image is that of a well, into which we peer, and to the surface of which we seek to draw the elusive shapes of the past. Nostalgia 'cannot resurrect the dead ... but it makes the dead speak and act as if they were alive. Having been brought to the surface from the well, which mirrors our faces whenever we lean over it, these dead are everything we desire to be'. While we imagine that what becomes visible in that long, receding tunnel, that well, is the past itself; we find that in actuality we are engaged in a narcissistic contemplation of the reflection of our own wishes and desires.

As happens so often, we can find this analysis of literature prefigured in literature itself. 'Shall I compare thee to a summer's day?' asks Shakespeare's *Sonnet XVIII*. No, is the answer, because the world of nature presents an image of change and extremity; while the beauty of the 'fair friend' to whom the sonnet is addressed is, by contrast, immutable and eternal:

> But thy eternall Sommer shall not fade,
> Nor loose possession of that faire thou ow'st,
> Nor shall death brag thou wandr'st in his shade,
> When in eternall lines to time thou grow'st,
>> So long as men can breath or eyes can see,
>> So long liues this, and this giues life to thee.[11]

If the immortality of the lover is guaranteed by the durability of these celebratory 'lines' of poetry, then that immortality is conditional on their survival. In turn, the poetry only survives so long as it is spoken and read; uttered by the breath of men, seen by living eyes. Men, however, cease to breathe, eyes lose their vision and poetry can be forgotten. This beauty is immortal only in so far as it is embodied in poetry; on condition that the poetry is read and subject to the availability of living readers.

There could be no better illustration of this truth than the subsequent fate of that poem, as it was recently deployed in a contemporary advertisement for women's clothes. In this representation, as in innumerable other vernacular quotations and lay readings, the poem delivered a modern heterosexual ideal of erotic escapism: the freedom of an open beach, occupied by a stereotype of feminine beauty: tall, blonde, barefoot but incongruously sheathed in a tight black cocktail dress. The image of desire produced by the original sonnet was, of course, quite different, since its object was not a feminine but a masculine beauty. The poem celebrated the beauty of a young man, described in 'Sonnet XX' as bearing 'a woman's face, by Nature's own hand painted'; created as a woman by Nature who then 'fell a-doting', equipped him with that 'one thing' that could make him an object of female desire ('prick'd out for women's pleasure') and thereby denied the poet his own proper erotic satisfaction. The 'desire' embodied in the poem is utterly unlike the 'desire' elicited by its modern appropriation. In the mirror of the poem's language, the modern reader is invited to discern a perfect reflection of his own desire. Meanwhile the poet, the young man, the painful and complex eroticism of those homosexual sonnets, are left to sink into the well without trace, dead indeed.

Now it is also true, of course, that another modern critic who might read the poem as a 'gay lyric', a celebration of homosexual love, is also finding in the poem's reflective surface a mirror-image of his own desire. And in my reading of the poem as self-consciously predictive of its own demise, I have offered a post-structuralist Shakespeare, who clearly must have had advance notice of the work of Roland Barthes and Jacques Derrida and Michel Foucault. Or, as Terry Eagleton puts it in *William Shakespeare*, 'though conclusive evidence is hard to come by, it is difficult to read Shakespeare without feeling that he was almost certainly familiar with Hegel, Marx, Neitschze, Freud, Wittgenstein and Derrida' [12]. In other words, in reading an old text we cannot disown our modern knowledge: consciously or unconsciously, we can interpret the language of the past only by translating it into a language we ourselves can understand.

&

In contemporary political debate over the teaching of English in schools, Shakespeare is routinely linked with other stipulations of the 'back-to-basics' educational policy, in particular the insistence on the need to teach and inculcate a mastery of grammar and spelling. The Conservative Education Secretary Gillian Shephard recently reaffirmed this linkage in addressing the 1994 Conservative Party Conference, where she 'urged the nation to take more pride in its literary heritage; and pledged to stamp out poor spelling and sloppy grammar'. 'Our English language' she said, 'is the tongue of Chaucer, Shakespeare, Milton'; hence schools must 'place the emphasis on the basics of grammar, spelling and punctuation'.

Standard English is here declared the common language of the literary inheritance, the language of Shakespeare, a language exemplifying a cultural continuity through the process of historical and political change. Language acquisition and literary education are seen as a seamless continuum, each an inevitable condition of the other, and literary and linguistic competence are tested against the same criteria. The ability to speak and write, clearly and confidently, Standard English, and the capacity to demonstrate an understanding of Shakespearean drama are thus closely linked in the National Curriculum for English, as in 'back-to-basics' political rhetoric.

Here is what might be styled The Great Shakespeare Spelling Test. A passage from the first edition of *King Lear*, published in 1608.[13]

Milke liuerd man
> That bearest a cheeke for bloes, a head for wrongs,
> Who hast not in thy browes an eye deseruing thine
> honour,
> From thy suffering, that not know'st, fools do those
> vilains pitty
> Who are punisht ere they haue done their mischiefe,
> Wher's thy drum? *France* spreds his banners in our
> noyseles land,

The spelling is not exemplary. 'liuerd'; 'bloes'; 'browes'; 'vilains'; 'pitty'; 'punisht'; 'Wher's'; 'spreds'; 'noyseles'; 'morall'. And the grammar and punctuation? 'From thy suffering, that not knows't, fools do those vilains pitty/Who are punished ere they have done their mischief'. On the strength of this, Shakespeare should go to the back of the class and study this corrected version, from a modernised edition.[14]

Milk-livered man,
> That bear'st a cheek for blows, a head for wrongs,
> Who hast not in thy brows an eye discerning
> Thine honour from thy suffering, that not know'st
> Fools do those villains pity who are punished
> Ere they have done their mischief. Where's thy drum?
> France spreads his banners in our noiseless land,

Spelling corrected, punctuation regularised and lines adjusted to make better grammatical sense to the modern editor. There we have Shakespearean English that can rather more convincingly simulate the 'Standard English' of modern educational policy. Unfortunately, it is not Shakespeare at all, but literally a modern translation.

The point is, of course, that the writing of Shakespeare cannot exemplify Standard English, since it was written long before the invention of Standard English.[15] The Right Honourable Mrs Shepherd needs to appreciate that if you really go back to basics, you are likely to find something quite different from what you wanted. On the other hand, the modernised Shakespeare text is there to persuade the conservative educationalist that it is history we see in the surface of the well, rather than a mirror-image of our own ideology.

The modern editor is not, however, content simply to correct and improve the original spelling and punctuation of the early modern text. Most modern editions entail a much higher level of interference and alteration. Take the example of Yorick, who is introduced, in the standard modern editions of *Hamlet* by way of a stage direction prescribing the gravedigger's action: '*He throws up a skull.*' You would search in vain for that stage direction in the original text on which this modern edition is based. Of the three extant original texts of Hamlet, only one – the real original or 'first edition', the so-called Bad Quarto of 1603, provides any stage direction at all, and there is no reference at all to a skull: '*He throwes up a shovel*'.[16] The authentic stage direction, which might possibly record an actual moment of stage business, was transferred in eighteenth century editions from the Bad to the Good text, from the Gravedigger to Hamlet, and emerged to read: *He throws up a skull*. The stage practice of using the skull as a key prop in the presentation of this scene does not go back to original performances of *Hamlet* (of which we know nothing other than the original texts and a few distant anecdotal recollections of performance). The theatrical tradition derives, in other words, from the altered and modernised eighteenth century texts, and not from the original. The originators then of even the most Shakespearean-seeming stage traditions are not dramatists or actors, but the relatively obscure scholars whose own interpretations acquire a substantial and independent potency when they are encoded within the apparently authoritative Shakespeare text.

It can, of course, be argued (and indeed has) that the presence or absence of a stage direction in no way precludes the centrality of the skull as an image within the action of this scene. That is true: but we still have to ask the question why is the skull there in the stage directions, rather than the shovel? Our dominant intellectual traditions clearly have a positive preference for the skull over the shovel. Not only is the skull an image of classical antiquity, the *memento mori* displayed at Roman banquets; it is also, as the repository of the brain, a symbol of the life of the mind. When we see Hamlet, in innumerable representations, face to face with the skull, what we see is an image of the princely poet-philosopher gazing stoically into the mysteries of life and death. Just as the title of the 'Globe' theatre laid pretensions, by analogy with the terrestrial globe, to universality, so the round skull was also an image of the world, as when Hamlet himself refers to his own tormented mind as 'this distracted globe'·

Meanwhile, the poor gravedigger with his shovel has lost his place in the story. Similarly, Thomas Hardy's Jude the Obscure stands outside the walls of an Oxford College and reflects on the ignorance of the 'hard readers' and 'high thinkers' within, of that exterior world of labour and endurance, the world of those workers without whose labours 'the hard readers could not read, and the high thinkers could not live'.[17] So the gravedigger's shovel, without which there would be no skull for the prince to contemplate, is edited out of the discourse of *Hamlet* in favour of an abstract and cerebral intellectualism.

The antitheses with which I'm playing – present and past, mask and face, reflection and reality, life and death – are not only deeply interconnected in this cultural analysis but start to emerge as binary oppositions, capable of reversing themselves and changing places with one another. The past appears to be something the present has already put there; the mask is just another expression of the face; reflection seems to conceal, rather than reveal, reality; and the dead are placed under interrogation and forced to speak a modern English that could never conceivably have been their authentic tongue.

These paradoxes are symbolised for me beautifully by the bronze statue of Hamlet in a Stratford park, where oxidisation of the metal has coated the living figure with a corruption of verdigris while the skull, the dead head of our cultural heritage, shines

with a living brilliance.[18] This recalls Stephen Greenblatt's finding
more intensity in the simulation, the 'formal, self-conscious
miming of life' accomplished by literature, than in any other
traces of a lost history. But another way of looking at the same
problem might be to regard the perfect, self-enclosed, polished
artefact as truly a dead object, *caput mortuum*, unless re-animat-
ed by the contingent traces of the life, the social and cultural
processes, that brought it into being and sustain its continuing
and continually changing existence. The first historical record
concerning John Shakespeare, the poet's father, is that he was
fined by the Stratford authorities for dumping his household shit
outside his own front door, rather than barrowing it down to the
town midden·. There is in Stratford so far as I know no statue of
John Shakespeare, shovel in hand, to commemorate that event.

Shakespeare's life is another territory of intense cultural conflict
and competition. The long-running controversy over Shakespeare's identity provides another example of the need for almost
everyone to claim and possess their own Shakespeare. These controversies are hardly at the centre of academic work on Shakespeare but certainly exercise some fascination over the public
imagination: an entire BBC programme in the 'Bard on the Box'
series was devoted to the competing claims of various candidates
on authorship of the Shakespeare canon. The kind of personal
appropriation represented by the 'Everybody is Shakespeare' slogan features very strongly here, in that rival claimants either are
(or claim to be) descended from their preferred candidate. An
American woman named Delia Bacon, who claimed direct
descent from the former Lord Chancellor, initially established the
Baconian hypothesis. The leading protagonist for the claim of
Edward de Vere, Earl of Oxford, is the present holder of that
name and title.

The curious thing about these controversies does not reside in the claims themselves but in the peculiar intensity of their focus on this particular writer. What does it matter, if the value lies in the writing, who actually penned it? The answer in fact has everything to do with the pre-eminent status accorded to Shakespeare, from the eighteenth century onwards, as the British national poet. If a writer is held to represent a nation, then people will expect him to perform that function effectively in their eyes. If there are within the nation radically different views of how the nation should be represented, it is likely that any one writer will be seen as a partial, inadequate or distorting image. Most of the rival claims on Shakespearean authorship were at the outset based simply on social class. It has been a matter of resentment that this great corpus of British national writing appears to have been produced by a man who had no university education and so a graduate alternative is found in Christopher Marlowe. It has been regarded as scandalous that the national poet should have been a product of the lower middle class and so aristocratic alternatives are sought in the Earl of Oxford or Frances Bacon, courtier, intellectual and statesman. It seems a national humiliation that Shakespeare not only emerged from relatively obscure and humble beginnings in a small Midlands market town but even retired back to them after completing the great Shakespearean *oeuvre*: so candidates of greater eminence and public visibility have been advanced, right up to Queen Elizabeth herself.

All this is clearly a process of myth making. It is difficult to accept, as Stanley Wells argued in that TV programme 'The Battle of Wills', that these claims are easily dismissed by reference to the self-evident 'reality' of Shakespeare's authorship: 'Shakespeare wrote Shakespeare'. Each rival candidature is a myth parallel to the most powerful myth of all, the construction of the Shakespearean reputation, and particularly its embodiment in the cultural apparatus of Stratford. It is probable that these plays were in any case written, or developed, collaboratively and the existence of variant texts indicates that they were certainly altered and influenced by people other than the author. But the real point is

that the 'Shakespeare' of today is the product of centuries of cultural development involving the participation of millions of contributors, and is in no way coterminous with any single historic
author: it is the world we see within that Shakespearean skull.

Other more fantastic but in some ways more interesting
myths around Shakespeare's life began to develop quite early in
the seventeenth century. There were, for example, the legends of
Shakespeare as a great drinker.[19] Like his friend Ben Jonson, one
antiquarian recorded, he 'loved a glass for the pleasure of society'.
Eighteenth-century travellers were shown on the road to the village of Bidford a crab-apple tree called 'Shakespeare's canopy',
under which, it was claimed, the poet found himself obliged to
rest after a particularly heavy afternoon. The story is that Shakespeare went to Bidford, a village familiarly known as 'Drunken
Bidford', in search of the famed local drinkers. He was told that
the Drinkers of Bidford were out but he could join the Sippers of
Bidford. The Sippers apparently belied their reputation since they
taught Shakespeare to drink deep ere he departed. This legend
can clearly be relocated in a historical origin: the stories circulated can all be traced back to the entrepreneurs who founded the
Stratford tourist industry, and to the innkeepers who cited local
drinking legends to their customers. Brewing was, and has
remained, a key local industry in Stratford. Beer-mats supplied
today by Flowers' brewery record that Shakespeare was 'extremely
fond of drinking hearty draughts of English ale'. The legend of
Shakespeare's licentious and liberated drinking retrospectively
endorse the exclusive trademark of a modern monopoly.[22]

A similar relationship between legend and history can be
found in the story of Shakespeare's youthful exploits as a poacher.
Early in the eighteenth century a tradition was established that
Shakespeare had been caught taking deer from the park at
Charlecote (near Stratford) of a local magistrate, Sir Thomas
Lucy. It was the severe punishments inflicted on the young
poacher for this offence – whipping is mentioned – that caused
him to flee to London. There, of course, he made his fortune and

later returned to Stratford a rich man and landowner thus (in later developments of the legend) exacting his revenge by writing scurrilous lampoons against Sir Thomas.

This story has the shape and structure of a folk-tale: Shakespeare appears here as a 'culture hero', exhibiting the classic narrative pattern of a misspent youth, the confrontation with a persecutor who thrusts the youth into exile, the hero's triumphant return and successful revenge.[23] The local topographical details proved a little shakey: sober eighteenth century scholars began to point out that at the time Sir Thomas Lucy did not have a park, and moreover had he had one, it would not have been stocked with deer. So the legend shifted its scene from Charlecote a few miles north to Fullbrook, where there were certainly deer that could conceivably have been poached by Shakespeare.

Modern enthusiasts have retained their fascination with this legend, even though sceptical about its veracity. Alice Fairfax-Lucy, descendant of Sir Thomas and occupant of Charlecote, put the position very clearly, again complicating our configurations of fantasy and reality:

> The portraits of Shakespeare are few and of debatable authenticity. In the shadowy throng of the Great he cuts a doubtful figure. But set him against the background of Charlecote warren or Fulbroke park some night near dawn, with dangerous moonlight whitening the turf, and there you have reality. Theft, capture, punishment, flight – these are all within the compass of ordinary experience.[20]

It is appropriate, in other words, that the life of a dramatist should itself be dramatic and again we find an author discovering a greater intensity in the dramatic simulation than in the more ordinary traces left by historical record.

We can, on the other hand, look to the historical record to find a counterbalancing narrative. In the poaching legend Shakespeare is given a role much like that of Robin Hood: an outlaw who represents an older and truer morality than that of the society that condemns him. Violating the enclosure of the aristocrat's park, transgressing the laws of private property that preserved game for specialist upper-class pleasures, Shakespeare dons the mantle of the free-born Englishman who was believed to have enjoyed the freedom and common ownership of both the land and its produce before the Norman Conquest. This prefigures the subsequent reclamation of that myth later in the seventeenth century, when the image of a free people satisfying their honest wants from a land in common ownership became a mobilising force in the English Revolution. An early manifestation of what became known as the 'Digger' movement occurred in Stratford in 1614: and Shakespeare was involved in it.

Not, however, any longer as a prototype of the freeborn Englishman claiming the fruits of God's earth for the common good but as the ally of an enclosing landlord. Shakespeare as a freeholder held land at Welcombe, near Stratford. Another local landowner, William Combe, promoted a scheme to enclose the common fields there. The Stratford council opposed the enclosure, as did the local people. Shakespeare signed a contract with Combe to protect his own boundaries and secure his tithes. Combe defied the Council, and proceeded with the enclosure, digging trenches and erecting hedge-mounds. Local tenants tried filling in the ditches and were violently attacked by Combe's men. The ditches were dug again by the enclosers; at night the women and children of Stratford defiantly filled them in (using, naturally, shovels). Shakespeare, it appears from the historical record, did nothing.[21]

Edward Bond constructed a play, *Bingo*, out of this episode.[22] The problem presented to Bond by this history was that of understanding how a writer capable of voicing the immensely humane sympathy for the poor and dispossessed that we find in *King Lear*:

> Poor naked wretches, wheresoe'er you are,
>   That bide the pelting of this pitiless storm,

> How shall your houseless heads and unfed sides
> Your looped and windowed raggedness, defend you
> From seasons such as these?[23]

could subsequently play an oppressive or at best uncaring role in a real social crisis. Bond has Shakespeare, unable to bear the extremity of this contradiction, kill himself in despair.

Bond's account, it could be argued, is just as much a fictionalisation as the legend of Shakespeare the poacher. There is some truth in this, although the latter has no historical authentication, while the former, however speculative, is based on evidence. I am less concerned, however, with historical authority, than with the co-existence within the tradition of such radically opposed appropriations of the Shakespearean biography. Is it possible for one Shakespeare to be everybody's? Or are some Shakespeares actually impossible to reconcile with those of others?

Despite the fact that Shakespeare is everybody's, and everybody is Shakespeare, this spectacle of confrontation and opposition between 'Shakespeare' and the people should not happen. But it frequently does, and there are some interesting recent examples. There are even occasions where groups of people actually say no to Shakespeare: a refusal which in our society, can evidently be regarded as a serious cultural crime.

In January of 1994 a media storm broke out around the headteacher of a Hackney primary school, who allegedly declined an opportunity for her children to receive discounted tickets for a performance of Prokefiev's ballet *Romeo and Juliet* at Covent Garden. Jane Brown was a much-respected professional, enjoying very strong parental support for her educational policies, and responsible for saving the school from a hit-list of 'problem' institutions. Her work in this context had been specifically praised by the Office for Standards in Education. The decision she made was the sort of administrative decision headteachers make every day:

whether or not the school could invest the money, time and effort involved in taking the children on an organised trip.

The controversy however crystallised around the particular reason she is alleged to have given for not taking up this offer: that '*Romeo and Juliet* was a story almost entirely about heterosexual love'. The tabloid press predictably sounded their alarm bells around 'political correctness' and its pernicious effects on education. The Prime Minister jumped in feet first, declaring in the Commons that 'political correctness is widely unpopular among parents who want their children to be taught in schools the basics of the English language and English history'. (It is not entirely clear how these aims could be furthered by means of a Russian ballet, based on an English version of an Italian story, with all the words taken out).

The media then unleashed what many described as a 'witch-hunt' against Jane Brown, who was forcibly 'outed' as a lesbian, and characterised by the tabloids as one whose imputed sexual 'deviance' had issued in the cultural deviance of objecting to Shakespeare. As the controversy got nastier, there were further allegations of corrupt and unethical professional conduct. The moral outrage co-ordinated by the press had its counterparts on the streets of Hackney, as Jane Brown began to receive death threats from some of her 'neighbours'.

The fundamental assumption in all this was that no one has the right to refuse Shakespeare. Here the idea of universal entitlement embodied in the National Curriculum appears in its coercive form: you will take your dose of 'everybody's Shakespeare', whether you like it or not. Shakespeare, like Guinness, is good for you; so to prevent children from gaining access to the Bard is, in this ideology, to deny them the healthy and life-giving cultural sustenance of their universal birthright. So on the one hand in this controversy we have Shakespeare, the national culture, the literary heritage, and normalcy; on the other, political correctness, loony-left educational policies, studying *Neighbours*, and deviancy.

The reality of this situation in practice hardly fitted the standard ideological model. To start with, was it actually 'Shakespeare'? In one sense Shakespeare was required, since the violent clamour of media protest against the teacher could only have been mobilised around the national Bard. Would the same outrage have arisen over ballet, very much a minority cultural interest? Or over Prokofiev, not by any means everybody's glass of vodka, rather than Shakespeare? Headlines such as 'Lesbian Teacher opposed to Ballet', or 'Pupils prevented from Partaking of Prokofiev' would not have carried the same weight.

Despite John Major's appeal to the silent majority, the parents of the school's children were 100 per cent supportive of their headteacher. To them the issue of the trip seemed less important than the teacher's record on educational standards, cultural integration and social harmony in a school environment of severe poverty and deprivation, racial tension, crime and violence. A Turkish father described Jane Brown as a teacher who 'cares': 'my boy doesn't get beaten up in the playground any more'. An African parent told reporters that Jane Brown had taken a real interest in her children, and created a school 'safe and nice with lots of learning'. In this community of intense social problems and powerful social solidarity, the Tory government's policy of 'parent-power' seriously backfired.

Even the teacher's particular judgement on the suitability of that show for her children deserves more serious consideration. Can we be so sure that the action of *Romeo and Juliet* would automatically function as an innocuous aesthetic experience or as the vehicle of sound moral values for primary school children? A 15-year old girl defies her parents to marry a man she chooses. What price family values? A young couple contracts a secret marriage, of doubtful legality, in clear transgression of parental authority and social convention. Aren't there enough teenage pregnancies in Hackney already?

More seriously, much of the action of *Romeo and Juliet* concerns urban violence and gang warfare, what would today be called organiseḋ bullying and systematic intimidation. Given that playground violence was the number one problem identified by *primary* Head Teachers in a survey published at the time of the Jane Brown controversy, doesn't Shakespeare at least have a case to answer? As one journalist put it, 'Jane Brown was worried that a ballet about family feuding, violence and death could upset some pupils. Away from Hackney that seems an implausible explanation; there it has a more authentic ring'.

Lastly, as we recall the complex sexuality of Shakespeare it seems perverse to use his name as the big stick of sexual normalcy with which to beat lesbians. Certainly when Jane Brown began to receive death threats from the cultural vigilantes of Hackney, possibly for the first time in history objection to Shakespeare came to be regarded as a capital crime.

One of my central concerns throughout has been this relationship between past and present. Is history something we discover or something we construct? Something we unearth, or something that is composed only in the act of exhumation? In the *Armed Forces Journal* for 1989,[24] appears a familiar yet dislocated image: The Globe Theatre, owned and managed by Shakespeare's Company, the Lord Chamberlain's men; the theatre in which Shakespeare himself held shares, and which was the site of production for many of his plays. It is underlined by a slogan: 'We helped protect The Globe in 1588'. Over the page it becomes apparent that the subject of that claim is Royal Ordnance, world-renowned supplier of defence systems. The advert unlocks the pun encoded in the theatre's name: in 1588, Royal Ordnance helped to protect the English state against the threat of the Spanish Armada, and therefore by implication defended that state's cultural apparatus.

Advertisment for Royal Ordnance. *Reproduced by kind permission of British Aerospace.* ▷

You Might Be Surprised By The Theatres We Play.

Since Shakespeare's work played at the Globe Theatre in 1588, Royal Ordnance's products have been in action in every major event of Britain's military history.

Today, we serve every theater of military operations. In the air. On land. And at sea.

We design and manufacture a complete range of weapon systems and sub-systems; as well as the reliable munitions which made our reputation.

And we're using this comprehensive experience in cooperation with American companies to meet the demanding requirements of the U.S. Army, Navy, Air Force, and Marines.

We are involved in everything from ground attack weapons and air-combat missiles to infantry weapons, artillery systems, specialist combat vehicles, missile systems, torpedo warheads, and mines.

Current program work is as diverse as insensitive munitions, low signature and liquid propellants, mine clearing line charges, intercom systems, future mortar systems and their ammunition, low recoil force guns, reactive armors, and lightweight howitzer developments.

After 400 years, Royal Ordnance still plays the Globe. All of it. Thanks to partnerships born in tradition and designed for excellence.

Partners in ▼═══ *Excellence*

ROYALORDNANCE

Defense systems, sub-systems and components

1101 Wilson Blvd., Suite 1200
Arlington, VA 22209 ● (703) 243-9599

A British Aerospace Company

By extension, Royal Ordnance protected the early modern world, the entire 'globe', making it safe for civilisation. The two images, one of the picturesque old theatre, the other of a sea and sky fizzling with missiles, were juxtaposed in sharp contrast: but the claim for the advert was for an unbroken continuity. Royal Ordnance's influence is now extended from its relatively parochial position in 1588, to a global theatre of military operations, encompassing the whole planet. This historical continuity consists in traditions of 'excellence' (their top-gun weapons are as top-class as Shakespeare's plays) and 'partnership' – from the early joint stock company represented by The Globe Theatre to the 'special relationship' between the United States and Britain.

There is however a very obvious discontinuity between these two historical moments. In 1588 Royal Ordnance was, as the name suggests, the private armourer of the British monarchy. Its function was to preserve that monarchy's power and to defend English interests. By the date of this advertisement, Royal Ordnance had been privatised by the Thatcher Government and (as indicated in the text of the advert) subsumed by British Aerospace. The global remit of the company is not therefore to defend a particular civilisation by the military support of its foreign policy but rather to promote the Anglo-American economy by supplying arms to the world. In the year this advert appeared, Royal Ordnance was exhibiting at the Baghdad Arms Fair, despite an ostensible arms embargo against Iraq.

The modern appropriation of Shakespearean iconography rests therefore on a defeating self-contradiction. Defensive technology defends itself by claiming the sanction and assimilating the values, of culture: 'We helped protect the Globe'. But it becomes difficult to sustain that civilising mission, when the 'theatre of military operations' recognises no national boundaries but consists in supplying deadly weapons to any nation with the money to pay for them,

This obfuscation of a real history, discontinuous and violent, by an emphasis on cultural homogeneity and historical continuity, is symptomatised by another detail in the text of the advert. It is not entirely accurate to claim that Royal Ordnance helped protect the Globe in 1588, for the simple reason that the Globe Theatre was not there to be protected. It was in fact constructed in 1599.

We are obviously confronted here with a manifest fictionalising of history, a processing of the past which once again renders it answerable to our own desires. That same Globe Theatre unfortunately burned down in 1613, its thatched roof ignited by the discharge of a canon, heralding a royal entrance in Shakespeare's play *The Life of Henry Eighth*. So while Royal Ordnance cannot claim to have protected the Globe in 1588, they could certainly take credit for having destroyed it in 1613.

෨

> Full fathom five thy father lies;
> Of his bones are coral made;
> Those are pearls that were his eyes
> Nothing of him that doth fade,
> But doth suffer a sea-change
> Into something rich and strange.

I recently read these lines, from Ariel's song in *The Tempest*, not at my desk or in a library, but travelling on the London underground's Northern Line, full-fathom five beneath Leicester Square. The poem appeared as one of London Transport's series of posters *Poems on the Underground*. There I was, on what travellers know as the 'Misery Line', my body impacted with the suffering flesh of a thousand fellow-passengers. I looked up, read the poster, and for a moment the Misery Line suffered a sea change. In that mysterious depth, a miraculous transformation took place. All that was perishable and corruptible mutated into the glowing phosphorescence of pearl and coral; all that was impermanent and decaying took on the immortality, the strange fragile beauty of living mineral. The dirt, the physical discomfort, the mental squalor of the Northern line, embellished by the words of Shakespeare, underwent a transformation into something rich and strange.

The train stopped at my station; I alighted; nothing had changed. The Northern line was still the Misery line. 'Poetry' wrote W.H. Auden, 'makes nothing happen' But also, 'it survives in the valley of its making'. I could easily have felt cheated and deceived but I found it more difficult to creep up on this poem and surprise it by revealing it as a cheap trick. Recalling Stephen Greenblatt's assertion that the self-conscious fictionality of poetry can 'anticipate and compensate for' the 'disappearance of the life that empowered it', I remembered that this poem knows it is a fiction. After all, Ferdinand's father is not dead at all; not drowned and rotten, but alive and well and living in that magic island subsequently identified as Bermuda. Ariel's song, compelling and beautiful as it is, is a pack of lies.

But still, I heard the music, whether it was true or false, i'the earth or i'the air. My understanding of it may have changed. Knowing that poetry 'makes nothing happen' I yet find myself admitting the strange tenacity with which it survives, 'in the valley of its making', to disclose new meanings from the seemingly inexhaustible phenomenon of Shakespeare.

Notes

⟡

Preface

1   Roland Barthes, *Mythologies* (1957), translated by Annette Lavers (London: Paladin, 1973). See also Graham Holderness, 'Agincourt 1944: readings in the Shakespeare Myth', *Literature and History*, 10:1 (1984), pp. 24-45. The latter essay features in the companion volume *Visual Shakespeare: essays in film and television*. (Hatfield: University of Hertfordshire Press, 2001)

2   Graham Holderness, ed., *The Shakespeare Myth* (Manchester: Manchester University Press, 1988), pp. xiv–xv.

3   As one reviewer put it, 'references are generally not to the industry of Shakespeare scholarship but to works in cultural, communication and interdisciplinary studies'. *Shakespeare Survey*, 42 (1990), p. 164.

4   *Appropriating Shakespeare: post-renaissance reconstructions of the works and the myth,* edited by Jean Marsden (Hemel Hempstead: Harvester Wheatsheaf, 1991).

5   Barbara Hodgdon, *The Shakespeare Trade: performances and appropriations* (Philadelphia: University of Pennsylvania Press, 1998), p. 194. Barbara Hodgdon's indebtedness to *The Shakespeare Myth* is made explicit in her own study of Stratford-upon-Avon (Chapter. 6) by reference to the essay printed here as Chapter Seven, 'Bardolatry': 'I am also interested in how the narratives of bardolatry, literary pilgrimage, leisure tourism, and theatrical entertainment are being combined, contested and revised. Whereas Graham Holderness writes a "cultural materialist's guide to Stratford-upon-Avon", I offer a guide to Stratford's theatre of material culture' (p. 194).

6   Stephen Clucas, 'Re-trod boards', *Times Higher Education Supplement*, 18 November 1988.

7   See *Political Shakespeare*, edited by Alan Sinfield and Jonathan Dollimore (Manchester: Manchester University Press, 1986, 2nd edition 1994); Terence Hawkes, *That Shakespeherian Rag* (London: Methuen, 1987); Terry Eagleton, *William Shakespeare* (Oxford: Blackwell, 1987).

8   *Shakespeare Survey*, 42 (1990), p. 164.

9.   The first academic unit set up for teaching and research in Cultural Studies was the Centre for Contemporary Cultural Studies, founded at Birmingham by Richard Hoggart. One of my first essays (on D.H. Lawrence) was published in the fifth issue of the centre's journal *Cultural Studies* (1974).

One: Production (1988)

First published as 'Shakespeare in Production', Gulliver (Deutsch-English Jahrbucher), Band 24, 'Shakespeare als Volkstheater', (1988), pp. 120–35.

1.   Terry Eagleton, 'Afterword' to Holderness, *The Shakespeare Myth*, p. 204.

2.   See for example Hawkes, *Shakespeherian Rag*; Eagleton, *Shakespeare*; Dollimore and Sinfield, *Political Shakespeare*; and *Alternative Shakespeares*, edited by John Drakakis (London: Methuen, 1986).

3.   David Hornbrook, address to NADATE conference, September, 1987.

4.   See Alan Sinfield, 'Royal Shakespeare: theatre and the making of ideology', in Dollimore and Sinfield, *Political Shakespeare*, 2nd edition, pp. 182–205; and Christopher J. McCullough, 'The Cambridge Connection', in Holderness, *The Shakespeare Myth*, pp. 112–21.

5.   I have discussed the use of alternative spaces in 'The Albatross and the Swan', *New Theatre Quarterly*, 14 (Spring 1988); and the potentialities of touring productions in *Shakespeare in Performance: The Taming of the Shrew* (Manchester: Manchester University Press, 1992).

6.   For further discussion see my essays 'Radical Potentiality and Institutional Closure: Shakespeare in film and television', in Dollimore and Sinfield, *Political Shakespeare*, 2nd edition, pp. 206–25, and 'Boxing the Bard: Shakespeare on Television', in Holderness, *The Shakespeare Myth*, pp. 173–89. The first reprinted in *Visual Shakespeare: essays in film and television*.

7.   Raymond Williams, *Television: Technology and Cultural Form* (London: Fontana, 1974), pp. 89–90.

8.   *Shakespeare in Perspective*, edited by Roger Sales (London: BBC/Ariel Books, 2 vols., 1982, 1985).

9. See also John Drakakis, 'Theatre, Ideology and Institution: Shakespeare and the roadsweepers', in Holderness, *The Shakespeare Myth*, pp. 24–41.

10. See Sam Wanamaker, interviewed by Graham Holderness, in Holderness, *The Shakespeare Myth*, pp. 16–23.

Two: Reproduction (1991)

First published as 'Production, Reproduction, Performance: marxism, history theatre', in *Uses of History: Marxism, Post-modernism in the Renaissance*, edited by Francis Barker, Peter Hulme and Margaret Iverson, (Manchester: Manchester University Press, 1991), pp. 153–78.

1. Walter Cohen, 'Political Criticism of Shakespeare', in *Shakespeare Reproduced*, edited by Jean Howard and Marion O'Connor (London: Methuen, 1987), pp. 18–46.

2. Simon Barker, 'Images of the Sixteenth and Seventeenth Centuries as a History of the present', in *Literature, Politics and Theory*, edited by Frances Barker, *et. alii.* (London, 1986), pp. 172–89; Dollimore and Sinfield, *Political Shakespeare*, 2nd edition, pp. 154–280; Holderness, *The Shakespeare Myth*; Hawkes, *Shakespeherian Rag*; Malcolm Evans, *Signifying Nothing* (Brighton: Harvester, 1986); Drakakis, *Alternative Shakespeares*.

3. Jean Howard and Marion O'Connor, 'Introduction' to Howard and O'Connor, *Shakespeare Reproduced*, pp. 15–16.

4. Marion O'Connor, 'Theatre of the Empire', in Howard and O'Connor, *Shakespeare Reproduced*, pp. 68–98.

5. Cohen, 'Political Criticism', p. 34.

6. Stephen Greenblatt, *Shakespearean Negotiations: the Circulation of Social Energy in Renaissance England* (Oxford: Oxford University Press, 1988).

7. Howard and O'Connor, 'Introduction' to *Shakespeare Reproduced*, p. 2.

8. See above, note 2.

9. Greenblatt, *Shakespearean Negotiations*, p. 1.

10. 'Bibliography of Political Studies of Shakespeare in the 1980s', appended to Cohen, 'Political Criticism', pp. 44–6.

Three: Performance (1985)

First published as 'Recyling History', from *Shakespeare, History* (Dublin: Gill and Macmillan, 1995).

1. Robert Hewison, *In Anger: Culture and the Cold War, 1945–60* (London: Weidenfeld and Nicolson, 1981), pp. 48–9.

2. *In Anger*, p. 49.
3. Michael Frayn, in *The Age of Austerity*, edited by Michael Sissons and Philip French (London: Hodder and Stoughton, 1963).
4. Quoted in *In Anger*, p. 55.
5. J. Dover Wilson and T.C Worsley, *Shakespeare's Histories at Stratford 1951* (London: Max Reinhardt, 1962).
6. Anthony Quayle, 'Foreword' to Wilson and Worsley, *Shakespeare's Histories at Stratford*, pp. xviii–ix.
7. Rosemary Anne Sissons, quoted in Wilson and Worsley, *Shakespeare's Histories at Stratford*, p. 55.
8. T.A. Jackson, quoted in Wilson and Worsley, *Shakespeare's Histories at Stratford*, p. 55.
9. See Sinfield, 'Royal Shakespeare' in Dollimore and Sinfield, *Political Shakespeare.*
10. T.C. Worsley in Wilson and Worsley, *Shakespeare's Histories at Stratford*, p. 31.
11. Ibid., photograph facing p. 10.
12. Buzz Goodbody's attempts to radicalise Shakespeare productions at Stratford's The Other Place involved changing the relations between actors and audience in this direction. See Dympna Callaghan, 'Buzz Goodbody: Directing for Change' in Marsden, *Appropriation of Shakespeare*, pp. 163–82.
13. Directed by Jane Howell as part of the BBC/Time-Life Shakespeare series, under the producership of Jonathan Miller. Broadcast 1983.
14. See Holderness, 'Radical Potentiality and Institutional Closure', and (with Christopher J. McCullough,) 'Boxing the Bard: the cultural politics of television Shakespeare', *Red Letters*, 18 (1986), pp. 23–33.
15. Maurice Charney, 'Shakespearean Anglophobia: the BBC-TV series and American Audiences', *Shakespeare Quarterly*, Vol. 31 (1980), p. 292.
16. Paul Johnson, '*Richard II*', in Sales, *Shakespeare in Perspective*, pp. 33–5.
17. Cedric Messina, 'Preface' to *The BBC-TV Shakespeare:' Richard II* ' (London: BBC/Ariel Books, 1978), pp. 7–8.
18. Jane Howell, quoted in Henry Fenwick. 'The Production' in *The BBC-TV Shakespeare Series: 'Henry VI, Part One'* (London: BBC/Ariel Books, 1983), pp. 22–3.
19. Ibid., p. 24.
20. Ibid., p. 29.
21. Fenwick in *BBC-TV 'Henry VI Part One'*, p. 25.
22. Howell quoted by Fenwick, in *BBC-TV 'Henry VI Part One'*, p. 24.
23. Ann Pasternack Slater, 'An Interview with Jonathan Miller', *Quarto*, 10 (September 1980), p. 9.
24. Ibid., p. 9. See also Jonathan Miller interviewed in Holderness, *The*

Shakespeare Myth, pp. 195–202.

25. Bertolt Brecht, quoted in *Brecht on Theatre*, edited by John Willett (London: Methuen, 1964), p. 71.

Four: National Culture (1991)

First published as '"What ish my nation": Shakespeare and National Identities', *Textual Practice*, 5/1 (1991), pp. 80–99.

1. Jack Tinker, *Daily Mail*, 29 March 1984. Reprinted in *London Theatre Record*, IV: 7 (1984), p. 270.

2. *Henry V*, directed by Kenneth Branagh, produced by Bruce Sharman, 1989; based on a 1984 production of the Royal Shakespeare Company, directed by Adrian Noble. My description 'widely celebrated' can be measured by the press reviews quoted later in this chapter; and see also the *Shakespeare on Film Newsletter*, 14:2, which cites in support of Robert F. Wilson's positive evaluation ('Henry V/Branagh's and Olivier's Choruses') a celebratory 'Chorus of critics' (pp. 1–2). Branagh received Academy Award nominations as best actor and best director.

3. Tom Hutchinson, *The Mail on Sunday*, 8 October 1989.

4. The phrase derives from D.H. Lawrence's poem 'Piano' (see note 5), but occurs more than once in the stage directions of Branagh's *Henry V* screenplay: see K. Branagh, *Henry V by William Shakespeare: a Screen Adaptation* (London: Chatto and Windus, 1989), p. 32.

5. D.H. Lawrence, 'Piano', in *Selected Poems of D.H. Lawrence*, edited by Keith Sagar (London: Penguin Books, 1972), p. 21.

6. Philip Larkin, 'Church Going', in *The Less Deceived* (London: Faber and Faber, 1957).

7. Raphael Holinshed, *Chronicles of England, Scotland and Ireland* (1577, 1587; New York: AMS Press, 1965), vol. 1, p. 443.

8. John Turner, 'King Lear', in Graham Holderness, Nick Potter and John Turner, *Shakespeare: the Play of History* (London: Macmillan, 1988), p. 92. See also Terence Hawkes, 'Lear's map: a general survey', *Deutsche Shakespeare-Gesellschaft West Jahrbuch* (1989), pp. 36–7.

9. Turner, 'King Lear', p. 93.

10. Cf. Seamus Heaney's poem, 'Act of Union', where a sexual relationship is linked metaphorically with the political connection of Britain and Ireland, coloniser and colonised: 'I grow older/Conceding your half-independent shore/Within whose borders now my legacy/Culminates inexorably'. See Seamus Heaney, *New Selected Poems 1966–1987* (London: Faber and Faber, 1990), pp. 74–5.

11. See Karl P. Wentersdorf, 'The conspiracy of silence in *Henry V*', *Shakespeare Quarterly*, 27 (1976), and Graham Holderness, '*Henry V*', in

Holderness, Potter and Turner, *Play of History*, pp. 70–2.

12. Branagh, in *Henry V: screenplay*, p. 12.

13. Ibid. pp. 35–6.

14. See Holderness, 'Agincourt 1944'; Graham Holderness, *Shakespeare's History* (Dublin, Gill and Macmillan, 1985), pp. 184–91; and Holderness, Potter and Turner, *Play of History*, pp. 72–9.

15. Philip French, *The Observer*, 8 October 1989.

16. Adam Mars-Jones, *The Independent*, 5 October 1989.

17. C. Tookey, *The Sunday Telegraph*, 8 October 1989.

18. Charles Wood, *Tumbledown* (London: Penguin Book, 1987).

19. Kenneth Branagh discusses his approach to the stage role of Henry V in *Players of Shakespeare*, edited by Philip Brockbank (Cambridge: Cambridge University Press, 1985), and in his own autobiography, *Beginning* (London: Chatto and Windus, 1989), pp. 137–9.

20. See Branagh, *Beginning*, pp. 141–4.

21. See Michael Quinn, 'Celebrity and the semiotics of acting', *New Theatre Quarterly*, VI: 22 (1990).

22. P. Lewis, *Sunday Times*, 10 September 1989.

23. Philip French, *The Observer*, 8 October 1989.

24. Adam Mars-Jones, *The Independent*, 5 October 1989.

25. P. Lewis, *Sunday Telegraph*, 24–30 September 1989.

26. B. Bamigboye, *Daily Mail*, 18 November 1989.

27. P. Lewis, *Sunday Times*, 10 September 1989.

28. Ian Johnstone, *Sunday Times*, 8 October 1989.

29. A. Lane, *The Independent*, 30 September 1989.

30. A. Bilson, *Sunday Correspondent*, 8 October 1989.

31. Alexander Walker, in the *London Evening Standard*, 25 May, 1989. Branagh himself ironically traced the roots of his career to a conjuncture of drama and sport: at school he was made captain of both rugby and football teams, 'I suspect for my innate sense of drama, I loved shouting theatrically butch encouragement to "my lads"' (Branagh, *Beginning*, p. 28).

32. P. Lewis, *Sunday Times*, 10 September 1989.

33. P. Lewis, *Sunday Telegraph*, 24–30 September 1989.

34. Quoted by P. Lewis, *Sunday Telegraph*, 24–30 September 1989.

35. R. Corliss, *The Times*, 13 November 1989, and Adam Mars-Jones, *The Independent*, 5 October 1989.

36. Raphael Samuel, 'Introduction: exciting to be English', in *Patriotism: the Making and Unmaking of National Identity*, edited by Raphael Samuel, vol. 1, *History and Politics* (London: Routledge, 1989), pp. xli–xlii, xxxix–xl.

37. Branagh, *Beginning*, p. 22.

38. Branagh, *Henry V: screenplay*, p. 111.
39. Quoted by P. Lewis, *Sunday Times*, 10 September 1989.
40. H. Davenport, *Daily Telegraph*, 5 October 1989.
41. See Branagh, *Beginning*, p. 20.
42. Ibid. p. 239.
43 See Holderness, *Shakespeare's History*, pp. 59–61.

Five: Heritage (1992)

First published as 'Shakespeare and Heritage', *Textual Practice*, 6/2 (1992), pp. 247–63.

1. *Facts About the Arts* 2 (London, Policy Studies Institute, 1986), estimated 213 million sightseeing visits in 1985, 67 million of these to historic buildings. The audience for the live arts in the same period is estimated at 39 million. Visits to galleries and museums in 1985 numbered 58 million, by contrast with 53 million visits to the cinema. On the other hand, visiting 'the heritage' is much cheaper: in 1987, £367 million was spent on the theatre and live entertainment (of which £129.6 million went on the West End theatres alone), while 'the heritage' took only £44.9 million of consumer spending. See 'Financing the Arts and Heritage', *Cultural Trends*, 1 (January 1989), p. 30.

2. This lack of conceptual definition co-exists however at the administrative level with a clear computation of the 'heritage' costs and responsibilities of such organisations as the National Trust, the Historic Buildings and Monuments commissions for Scotland and Wales, English Heritage and the Department of the Environment; see *Cultural Trends*, 1 (1989).

3. Patrick Wright, *On Living in an Old Country: the National Past in Contemporary Britain* (London: Verso, 1985), p. 183.

4. See Robert Hewison, *The Culture Industry: Britain in a Climate of Decline* (London: Methuen, 1987); and Wright, *On Living in an Old Country*.

5. Donald Horne, *The Great Museum: the Re-presentation of History* (London: Pluto Press, 1985).

6. There is, of course, no doubt as to the 'authenticity' of the stones themselves, though it should be added that contemporary Avebury is in itself to some degree a reconstruction. 'Little more than 300 years ago, the Wessex downland was littered with so many massive stones that it was difficult to identify a prehistoric monument at Avebury. And even when the presence of great stone settings was recognised, it was hard to com-

prehend their ground plan with so much modern activity taking place among them. Parts of the great circle seem to have been cultivated, and the stones themselves were overthrown and buried to remove obstacles to the plough. Other stones were broken up by using a combination of fire and water to provide building material for the local inhabitants. Much of the modern village is constructed from the remains of the pre-historic monument ... it is difficult to realise how little of it is original' (Richard Bradley, 'No stones left unturned', *Times Higher Education Supplement* [5 July 1991], p. 22.) See also *Avebury Reconsidered; from the 1660s to the 1990s*, edited by Peter J. Ucko, Michael Hunter, Alan J. Clark, and Andrew David (London: Harper Collins, 1990).

7.   See Drakakis, 'Theatre, ideology and institution', in Holderness, *The Shakespeare Myth*, pp. 24–41.

8.   See Graham Holderness, 'A spear carrier's charter', *Times Higher Education Supplement* (29 April 1988), p. 13.

9.   See Drakakis, 'Theatre, ideology and Institution', p. 28.

10.   See Sam Wanamaker interviewed by Graham Holderness in Holderness, *The Shakespeare Myth*, pp. 22–3.

11.   Waldemar Januszczak, 'Shine of steel', *The Guardian*, 17 September 1986.

12.   Patrick Wright, *On Living in an Old Country*, p. 76.

13.   See Chapter 3, 'Performance', and for the Festival of Britain in general, see Hewison, *In Anger*.

14.   English Heritage was established by the National Heritage Act, 1983, and launched in April 1984, taking over the functions of the Directorate of Ancient Monuments and Historic Buildings, the Historic Buildings Council and the Ancient Monuments Board. It is the responsibility of English Heritage to advise on the listing of buildings and the scheduling of monuments, and to dispense grants for rescue archaeology and building conservation.

15.   Quoted in the *London Evening Standard*, 12 June 1989.

16.   Quoted in Christine Eccles, *The Rose Theatre* (London, Nick Hern Books, 1990), p. 231.

17.   One possible precedent for this spontaneous feminisation was the recovery in 1982 of the wreck of the Tudor ship, the *Mary Rose*. Inviting comparison with Cleopatra at the Battle of Actium, this female vessel chickened out of Anglo-French hostilities by sinking in Portsmouth Harbour. The raising of the wreck was imagined as the conquest and legitimisation of a coy and wayward female by the masculine powers of maritime archaeology, engineering and conservation technology. See Patrick Wright, *On Living in an Old Country*, and Simon Barker, 'Images of the sixteenth and seventeenth centuries'. For Prince Philip's oak see the *Southwark Globe*, Spring 1987, p. 1.

18. C. Walter Hodges, quoted in Eccles, *Rose Theatre*, p. 146.

19. *The Globe* (Autumn 1989), p. 2.

20. Stonehenge is the best-known example of a heritage site being destroyed more effectively by tourism than by the processes of time. The ancient hilltop fort of Navan in Co. Armagh, once the seat of the kings of Ulster, is also threatened by the Northern Ireland Department of Environment's granting of outline planning permission for a visitors' centre 300 metres below the outlying ramparts. Archaeologists claim the projected centre would lead to destruction of the monument. See *The Guardian*, 8 May 1991.

21. Laurence Olivier, quoted in Eccles, *Rose Theatre*, p. 175.

22. Ian McKellen, quoted in Eccles, *Rose Theatre*, p. 200.

23. Eccles, *Rose Theatre*, p. 169

24. See Chapter Seven, 'Bardolatry'.

25. Cited in F.C. Halliday, *The Cult of Shakespeare* (London, 1957), pp. 67–8.

26. See Chapter Seven, 'Bardolatry'.

27. See Peter Reynolds, 'Community theatre: carnival or camp?', in *The Politics of Theatre and Drama*, edited by Graham Holderness (London: Macmillan, 1991).

28. See Alan Swingewood, *The Myth of Mass Culture* (London: Macmillan, 1987), pp. 12–18.

29. Details from publicity leaflet, *The Tempest*, Phoebus Cart in association with The Scottish Ballet.

30. Quoted in the *London Evening Standard*, 7 June 1991.

Six: Shakespeare's England (1997)

First published as 'Shakespeare's England': Britain's Shakespeare', (with Andrew Murphy), in *Shakespeare and National Culture*, edited by John Joughin, (Manchester: Manchester University Press, 1997), pp. 19–41.

1. From Samuel Johnson's edition of Shakespeare (London, 1765), p. lvii.

2. See Allan Bloom, *The Closing of the American Mind* (New York: Simon and Schuster, 1987).

3. Terry Eagleton, *Literary Theory: An Introduction* (Oxford: Basil Blackwell, 1983).

4. Patrick Wintour and Stephen Bates, 'Major goes back to the old values', *The Guardian*, 9 October 1993, p. 6. There is a certain odd irony at the heart of Major's parodic adoption of this 'demotic' register – he himself has few academic qualifications and is not university-educated, a fact much trumpeted on his accession to the leadership of the Conservative Party and during the course of the 1992 General Election, when he was

presented as the embodiment of a modern, democratic, 'class-less' conservatism.

5. The letter was originally drafted by a group of twenty-one professors of English, including Professors Alan Sinfield, Lisa Jardine and Catherine Belsey. It was published in *The Times Higher Education Supplement*, 20 November, 1992. Subsequently, the letter was circulated to English departments throughout the country and garnered a further five hundred signatures. The original letter, together with a list of the further signatories, is reprinted in the *THES*, 11 June, 1993, p. 15. This same issue of the *THES* also includes a 'Perspective special', consisting of a selection of articles on 'the forces fighting in the field of English', p. 17.

6. *The Observer*, 22 August 1993, pp. 37–8. For further articles of a similar kind, see 'To see or not to see', 'Brush up your Shakespeare' and 'Bard folk' in *The Guardian* (2), 13 October 1994, pp. 2–4; and 'Was Shakespeare really a genius?' in *The Guardian* (2), 8 March 1995, pp. 10–11.

7. See Dollimore and Sinfield, *Political Shakespeare*; Drakakis, *Alternative Shakespeares*; Holderness, *The Shakespeare Myth*; Gary Taylor, *Reinventing Shakespeare*; Michael Bristol, *Shakespeare's America, America's Shakespeare* (London: Routledge, 1990); Marsden, *The Appropriation of Shakespeare*; and Michael Dobson, *The Making of a National Poet: Shakespeare, Adaptation and Authority, 1660–1769* (Oxford: Clarendon Press, 1992).

8. Ann Thompson, Thomas L. Berger, A.R. Braunmuller, P. Edwards and Lois Potter, *Which Shakespeare? A User's Guide to Editions* (Milton Keynes: Open University Press, 1992).

9. *William Shakespeare: The Complete Works (Compact Edition)*, edited by Stanley Wells and Gary Taylor (Oxford: Clarendon Press, 1988), p. 25.

10. On the significance of Malone's edition as a watershed text in the editorial tradition, see Margreta de Grazia's compelling and persuasive *Shakespeare Verbatim: The Reproduction of Authenticity and the 1790 Apparatus* (Oxford: Clarendon Press, 1991).

11. Fredson Bowers, *Textual and Literary Criticism* (Cambridge: Cambridge University Press, 1966), p. 8.

12. Fredson Bowers, *Bibliography and Textual Criticism* (Oxford: Clarendon Press, 1964), p. 8.

13. The one possible exception is the 'Hand D' contribution to the manuscript of 'The Book of Sir Thomas More', but even this is questionable – see Scott McMillin, *The Elizabethan Theatre and 'The Book of Sir Thomas More'* (Ithaca: Cornell University Press, 1987), especially pp. 135–59.

14. Graham, Holderness and Bryan Loughrey, 'Text and stage: Shakespeare,

bibliography, and performance studies', *New Theatre Quarterly*, 9:34 (1993), pp. 187–8. Reprinted in companion volume *Textual Shakespeare: essays in bibliography* (Hatfield: University of Hertfordshire Press, 2002).

15. Charlton Hinman, *The First Folio of Shakespeare* (New York: Norton, 1968), p. xi. This text is, in itself, a most extraordinary example of conflation in action. Setting out to produce a facsimile edition of the 1623 Folio, Hinman quickly abandoned the established practice of reproducing one of the particular extant copies of the text, opting instead to produce a text which consisted of an assemblage of the best pages drawn from thirty of the eighty copies of the First Folio held in the collection of the Folger Shakespeare Library in Washington DC. He thus 'sought' as he observes, 'to give concrete representation to what [had] hitherto been only a theoretical entity, an abstraction: the First Folio' (p. xxii).

17. Fredson Bowers, *On Editing Shakespeare and the Elizabethan Dramatists* (Philadelphia: University of Pennsylvania Library, 1955), p. 35. The tone of Bowers' comment on literary critics is characteristic. Elsewhere, in *Textual and Literary Criticism*, he writes: 'it is still a current oddity that many a literary critic has investigated the past ownership and mechanical condition of his second-hand automobile, or the pedigree and training of his dog, more thoroughly than he has looked into the qualifications of the text on which his critical theories rest' (p. 5).

18. For a good example of the great early summation of such work, see W.W. Greg's *The Shakespeare First Folio: Its Bibliographic and Textual History* (Oxford, Clarendon, 1955).

19. It is a mark of this theatrical emphasis that the Oxford texts are heavily supplemented with speculative stage directions, and that the visual representation of the act and scene divisions has been diminished in order to suggest, as far as possible, a single continuous performance text.

20. McMillin, *The Elizabethan Theatre*, p. 154.

21. Ibid., p. 154.

22. Jerome J. McGann, *A Critique of Modern Textual Criticism* (Chicago: University of Chicago Press, 1983; Charlottesville: University of Virginia Press, 1992), p. 21.

23. Jerome J. McGann, *The Textual Condition* (Princeton: Princeton University Press, 1991), p. 21.

24. Roland Barthes, 'The death of the author', in *Image Music Text*, translated by Stephen Heath (London: Flamingo, 1984), p. 147.

25. Michel Foucault, 'What is an author?' in *The Foucault Reader*, edited by Paul Rabinow (New York: Pantheon, 1984), pp. 118–19.

26. Walter Benjamin, 'The work of art in the age of mechanical reproduc-

tion', in *Illuminations,* translated by Harry Zohn (New York: Schocken), 1969, p. 221.

27. For the origins of this division, see Alfred W. Pollard, *Shakespeare Folios and Quartos: A Study in the Bibliography of Shakespeare's Plays, 1594–1685* (London: Methuen, 1909), especially p. 80.

28. For the first outlining of a theory of memorial reconstruction, see the introduction to W.W. Greg's edition of *The Merry Wives of Windsor* (Oxford: Clarendon Press, 1910), pp. xxvii–xli.

29. McLeod, 'The marriage of good and bad quartos', p. 421.

30. Jonathan Goldberg, 'Textual Properties', *Shakespeare Quarterly,* 37:2 (1986), p. 213. McGann has also noted this intersection, observing in the Preface to the 1992 edition of his *Critique* that: 'Whereas textual theory had previously been the province and interest of a small group of scholars who generally confined themselves to technical and editorial studies it is now one of the liveliest arenas of general critical studies. Theory, textual scholarship, and interpretation no longer operate in their separate but (un)equal worlds' (p. xxii).

31. Work of this kind has already been undertaken by a number of scholars. See in particular Annabel Patterson's chapter on the texts of *Henry V* in *Shakespeare and the Popular Voice* (Oxford: Blackwell, 1989), and Leah Marcus, 'Leveling Shakespeare: local customs and local texts', *Shakespeare Quarterly,* 42:2 (1991), pp. 168–78.

32. See, for example, Sinfield and Dollimore's 'Foreword' on cultural materialism in their Manchester University Press *Cultural Politics* series, where they note that, in cultural materialist analysis, '"high culture" is taken as one set of signifying practices among others'.

Seven: Bardolatry (1988)

First published as "Bardolatry: or, the Cultural Materialist's guide to Stratford-upon-Avon', from *The Shakespeare Myths,* (Manchester: Manchester University Press, 1988).

1. F.J. Furnivall, 'Introduction' to his edition of Gervinus' *Commentaries* (1875); quoted in Louis Marder, *His Exits and Entrances: the Story of Shakespeare's Reputation* (London: John Murray), 1963, p. 251.

2. See Ivor Brown and George Fearon, *Amazing Monument: a Short History of the Shakespeare Industry* (London: Heinemann, 1939), pp. 9–11.

3. See Brown and Fearon, *Amazing Monument,* p. 140.

4. Deelman, *Shakespeare Jubilee,* p. 15; Brown and Fearon, *Amazing Monument,* p. 28.

5. See Christian Deelman, *The Great Shakespeare Jubilee* (London:

Michael Joseph, 1964), p. 34; and Brown and Fearon, *Amazing Monument*, p. 28.

6. Deelman, *Shakespeare Jubilee*, pp. 34–5.

7. See Thomas Davies, *Memoirs of the Life of David Garrick* (London, 1781), vol. 2, p. 218; Brown and Fearon, *Amazing Monument*, p. 57; and Marder, *Exits and Entrances*, pp. 235–6.

8. Robert Bell Wheler, *History and Antiquities of Stratford-upon-Avon* (Stratford, 1806), p. 138; Brown and Fearon, *Amazing Monument*, pp. 58–60; Marder, *Exits and Entrances*, pp. 236–7; and Martha Winburne England, *Garrick's Jubilee* (Bowling Green, Ohio: Ohio State University Press, 1964), p. 9.

9. Deelman, *Shakespeare Jubilee*, pp. 48–9.

10. Wheler, *Antiquities*, pp. 137–8.

11. Brown and Fearon, *Amazing Monument*, pp. 66–7.

12. Ibid., p. 146.

13. William Smith, *A New and Complete History of the County of Warwick* (1829), quoted in Brown, *Amazing Monument*, p. 149.

14. Washington Irving gives an unrivalled account of Widow Hornby in his essay 'Stratford-on-Avon'; see 'Sketch Book', edited by Haskell Springer, in *The Complete Works of Washington Irving* (Boston: Twayne Publishers, 1978), pp. 210–211. See also Brown and Fearon, *Amazing Monument*, pp. 151–2; and Marder, *Exits and Entrances*, pp. 241–3.

15. See Deelman, *Shakespeare Jubilee*, p. 6.

16. Levi Fox, *The Shakespearean Properties* (Stratford-upon-Avon: Shakespeare Birthplace Trust, 1981).

17. Wilfrid J. Osborne, *Anne Hathaway's Cottage* (Stratford-upon-Avon: Shakespeare Birthplace Trust, 1951), p. 4.

18. Roland Barthes, *Mythologies* (1957), translated by Annette Lavers (London: Paladin, 1973), p. 76.

19. See Horne, *The Great Museum*.

20. See Susan Sontag, *On Photography* (1977; Harmondsworth: Penguin, 1979).

21. See E.K. Chambers, *The Elizabethan Stage* (Oxford: Oxford University Press, 1923), vol. 2, pp. 367–9.

22. John Stow, *A Survey of London*, quoted in Chambers, *Elizabethan Stage*, vol. 2, p. 263.

23. Fynes Moryson, *Itinerary* (1617); quoted in Andrew Gurr, *The Shakespearean Stage, 1574–1642* (Cambridge: Cambridge University Press, 2nd edition, 1980), p. 10.

24. Thomas Heywood, *An Apology for Actors* (London, 1612), sig. F3.

25. See Graham Holderness, *Shakespeare's History* (Dublin: Gill and Macmillan, 1985), pp. 158–60. Ann Jennalie Cook's 'privileged playgoer'

thesis, notwithstanding its one-sided distortion of the evidence, obviously has implications for this argument: see her *The Privileged Playgoers of Shakespeare's London* (Princeton, NJ: Princeton University Press, 1981); and for a corrective critique, Martin Butler, *Theatre and Crisis* (Cambridge, Cambridge University Press, 1984), pp. 293–306.

26.   See Alfred Harbage, 'Shakespeare as a culture hero', *Aspects of Shakespeare* (Oxford: Oxford University Press, 1966).

27.   See, e.g. *The Sunday Times*, 24 November 1985.

28.   See for example correspondence in the *Times Literary Supplement*, 24 and 31 January 1986.

29.   See Erica Sheene and Jeremy Maule, 'Shall I Die?', *Times Literary Supplement*, 17 January 1986.

30.   Michel Foucault, *Language, Counter-memory, Practice* (Oxford: Blackwell, 1977), p. 124.

31.   Hawkes, *Shakespeherian Rag* (London, Methuen, 1986), pp. 75–6.

Eight: Shakespearean Features (1991)

First published as Shakespearean Features', (with Bryan Loughrey), in *Appropriating Shakespeare: Post-Renaissance Reconstructions of the Works and the Myth*, editied by Jean Marsden, (Hemel Hempstead: Harvester Wheatsheaf, 1991, pp. 183–201).

1.   The first part of *The Return to Parnassus*, in *The Three Parnassus Plays*, edited by J.B. Leishman (London: Nicholson and Watson, 1949), pp. 192–3.

2.   W.B. Yeats, 'A General Introduction for my Work' (1937), *Essays and Introductions* (New York: Macmillan, 1961), p. 10.

3.   George Orwell, 'Charles Dickens', in *Collected Essays, Journalism and Letters*, vol. 1, 'An Age Like This, 1920–1940', edited by Sonia Orwell and Ian Angus (London: Harcourt Brace Jovanovich, 1968), p. 460.

4.   Ben Jonson, 'To the memory of my beloued, The Avthor Mr. William Shakespeare: And what he hath left vs', facing the Droeshout title-page engraving to the First Folio (*Mr William Shakespeares Comedies, Histories and Tragedies* [London, 1623]).

5.   Anne Barton, *Ben Jonson, Dramatist* (Cambridge: Cambridge University Press, 1984), p. 3.

6.   Gary Taylor, *Reinventing Shakespeare*, (New York: Weidenfield and Nicolson, 1989) p. 6.

7.   A.L. Rowse, *The English Spirit: Essays in History and Literature* (London: Macmillan, 1945, 1966), pp. 5–6.

8.   Entry in the Stratford Visitors' Book, cited in Samuel Schoenbaum,

Shakespeare's Lives (New York: Oxford University Press, 1970), p. 187.

9. The Chandos portrait is the only other serious contender. For details of it and other so-called primary portraits of Shakespeare see *The Reader's Encyclopaedia of Shakespeare*, edited by Oscar James Campbell and Edward G. Quinn (New York: Cromwell, 1966), pp. 652–6; Samuel Schoenbaum, *William Shakespeare: Records and Images* (London: Scolar Press, 1981), chap. 5; and David Piper, *The Image of the Poet: British Poets and Their Portraits* (Oxford: Clarendon Press, 1982), passim.

10. Schoenbaum, *Shakespeare's Lives*, pp. 13–14.

11. For details of this portrait see Bryan Loughrey and Neil Taylor, 'Shakespeare and Jonson at Chess?', *Shakespeare Quarterly*, 34:4 (Winter 1983), pp. 440–8.

12. Letter to M.H. Spielman, dated 10 September 1934, and now in the Folger Shakespeare Library, Washington DC.

13. Unpublished Appendix IX of *Shakespeare's Imagery*, pp. 385–6, in the Folger Shakespeare Library. Spurgeon was eventually persuaded that to use the chess portrait as her cover illustration might distract from the force of her argument.

14. We are reminded of the fact that Charlie Chaplin is reputed to have entered a 'Charlie Chaplin look-alike' competition and to have been placed third. On 23 April 1988 the International Shakespeare Globe Trust organised a 'Shakespeare look-alike' competition in which foreheads figured prominently. The Trust celebrated the Bard's 1990 birthday with a huge banner of the Droeshout engraving held aloft for aerial photography by more than sixty people who share the Shakespeare name.

15. Recent restoration has revealed it to be a genuine contemporary portrait of Sir Hugh Hammersley, Lord Mayor of London, strategically falsified.

16. Details of the contract are contained in the files of the portrait's current owner.

17. Hawkes, *Shakespeherian Rag*, p. 75.

18. Epistle prefixed to the 1607 quarto of *Volpone*.

19. See *Ben Jonson*, edited by H. Hereford and Percy and Evelyn Simpson (Oxford: Clarendon Press, 1952), vol. III, p. ix.

20. Cited in Samuel Schoenbaum, *Shakespeare: the Globe and the World* (New York: Oxford University Press, 1979), p. 174.

21. 'To the Great Variety of Readers', prefatory matter to the First Folio, 1623.

22. Roger Chartier, 'Meaningful Forms', *Liber*, 1, p. 8. Chartier's argument derives from D.F. McKenzie's pioneering *Bibliography and the Sociology of Texts* (London: British Library, 1986).

23. See J. Dover Wilson, *The Essential Shakespeare* (Cambridge: Cambridge University Press, 1932), p. 6.

24. The Folger Shakespeare Library has a Victorian 'Bible-Shakespeare Calendar', the cover of which features a Shakespearean visage assimilated to the traditional iconographic conventions used for representing Christ. In contrast, most cartoon illustrations of Shakespeare resemble, if they are not derived from, Picasso's famous sketch. The bust used in Batman is derived ultimately from the Scheemakers statue.

25. Deelman, The *Great Shakespeare Jubilee*, pp. 69–70.

Nine: Everybody's Shakespeare (1994)

1. See the 1994 programme for the International Festival, *Everybody's Shakespeare*, The Barbican Centre and Royal Shakespeare Company (October /November 1994). 'Everybody's Shakespeare is the first event of its kind in this country and probably the world: an international multi-disciplined celebration of the work and influence of Shakespeare' (Adrian Noble).

2. First Folio prefatory poem 'To the memory of my beloued, The Avthor Mr. William Shakespeare: And what he hath left vs' (1623).

3. Ronald Carter, *The National Curriculum for English* (London: British Council, 1991) refers to 'the importance of Shakespeare and of authors who represent a distinct cultural heritage' (p. 21).

4. See Note 2 above.

5. Anthony Burgess, *Shakespeare* (1970, London: Penguin, 1972), p. 261.

6. The series is discussed in 'Boxing the Bard' (1988), in *Visual Shakespeare*.

7. James Wood, *London Review of Books*, 22 March 1990, quoted in Dollimore and Sinfield, *Political Shakespeare*, 2nd edition, p. 258–9.

8. T. S. Eliot, 'Little Gidding' in *Collected Poems 1909–1962* (London: Faber and Faber, 1963), p. 215.

9. Greenblatt, *Shakespearean Negotiations*.

10. Agnes Heller, *A Philosophy of History in Fragments* (Oxford: Blackwell, 1993), p. 40.

11. *Shake-Speares Sonnets* 1609 (London and Menston: Scolar Press Facsimile, 1968), B4v.

12. Eagleton, *Shakespeare*, pp. ix–x.

13. *M. William Shak-Speare's King Lear: The First Quarto 1608*. Shakespeare-Quarto Facsimiles, No.33 (London: C. Praetorius, 1885), p. 57.

14. *The First Quarto of King Lear*, edited by Jay L Halio (Cambridge: Cambridge University Press, 1990), pp. 96–7.

15. See 'Shakespeare's England' in this volume.

16. *The Tragicall Historie of Hamlet Prince of Denmarke* 1603, edited by Graham Holderness and Bryan Loughrey (Hemel Hempstead: Harvester Wheatsheaf, 1992), p. 91.

17. Thomas Hardy, *Jude the Obscure* (1896, London: Penguin, 1978), p. 166.

18. See Chapter Two, 'Bardolatry'.

19. *British Magazine* (1762), an anonymous 'Letter from the place of Shakespeare's Nativity'. Quoted in Samuel Schoenbaum *Shakespeare: A Compact Documentary Life* (Oxford: Oxford University Press 1987), p. 96. See also pp. 95–7 and 259.

20. Schoenbaum, *Life*, pp. 108–9.

21. Ibid. pp. 281–5.

22. Edward Bond, *Bingo* in *Plays 3: Bingo, The Fool, The Woman, Stone* (London: Methuen, 1987).

23. *The Tragedy of King Lear*, edited by Stanley Wells and Gary Taylor (Oxford: Oxford University Press, 1986), 3.4. 28–32.

24. See Alan Sinfield, *Faultlines: Cultural Materialism and the Politics of Dissident Reading* (Oxford: Clarendon Press, 1992), Fig.1, and p. 1. I am indebted to Alan Sinfield's discussion of this image.

Bibliography

The following books and articles, published since 1968, address in whole or part issues – theoretical, critical, social or political – appertaining to 'The Shakespeare Myth' school of criticism.

Althusser, Louis. 'Ideology and Ideological State Apparatuses (Notes towards an Investigation)', in *Lenin and Philosophy and Other Essays*, translated by Ben Brewster, London, New Left Books, 1971

Apple, Michael W. (ed.) *Cultural and Economic Reproduction in Education: Essays on Class, Ideology and the State*, London, Routledge, 1982

Barker, Francis, Peter Hume and Margaret Iverson (eds). *Uses of History: Marxism, post-modernism and the Renaissance*, Manchester, Manchester University Press, 1991

Barker, Francis. *The Culture of Violence: Essays on Tragedy and History*, Manchester, Manchester University Press, 1993

Barthes, Roland. 'The Death of the Author', 1968, in *Image – Music – Text*, translated and edited by Stephen Heath, London, Fontana, 1977, pp. 142-8

Bradshaw, Graham. *Misrepresentations: Shakespeare and the Materialists*, Ithaca and London, Cornell University Press, 1993

Belsey, Catherine. 'Re-reading the Great Tradition', in Widdowson, Peter (ed.) *Re-Reading English*, London, Methuen, 1985

Belsey, Catherine. *The Subject of Tragedy: Identity and Difference in Renaissance Drama*, London, Methuen, 1985

Benjamin, Walter. 'The work of art in the age of mechanical reproduction', in *Illuminations*, trans. Zohn, Harry, New York, Schocken, 1969

Bristol, Michael. *Carnival and Theatre: Plebian Culture and the Structure of Authority in Renaissance England*, London, Methuen, 1985

Bristol, Michael. *Shakespeare's America, America's Shakespeare*, London, Routledge, 1990

Burckhardt, Sigurd. *Shakespearean Meanings*, Princeton, Princeton University Press, 1968

Butler, Martin. *Theatre and Crisis*, Cambridge, Cambridge University Press, 1984

Calderwood, James. *Shakespearean Metadrama*, Minneapolis, University of Minnesota Press, 1971

Charney, Maurice. 'Shakespearean Anglophobia: the BBC-TV series and American audiences', *Shakespeare Quarterly*, Vol. 31, 1980. pp. 287–92

Charney, Maurice (ed.). *'Bad' Shakespeare: Revaluations of the Shakespeare Canon*, London, Associated University Presses, 1988

Cohen, Walter. *Drama of a Nation: Public Theater in Renaissance England and Spain*, Ithaca, NY, Cornell University Press, 1985

Dash, Irene. *Wooing, Wedding, and Power: Women in Shakespeare's Plays*, New York, Columbia University Press, 1981

Davies, Tony. 'Education, ideology and literature', *Red Letters*, No. 7, n.d. pp. 4–15

Dobson, Michael. *The Making of a National Poet: Shakespeare, Adaptation and Authority, 1660–1769*, Oxford, Clarendon, 1992

Dollimore, Jonathan. *Radical Tragedy: Religion, Ideology and Power in the Drama of Shakespeare and his Contemporaries*, Brighton, Harvester Press, 1984

Dollimore, Jonathan. 'Shakespeare, Cultural Materialism, Feminism and Marxist Humanism', in *New Literary History* 21, 1990, pp. 471–94

Dollimore, Jonathan and Sinfield, Alan (eds). *Political Shakespeare*, Manchester, Manchester University Press, 1985, 2nd edition with additional chapters, 1994

Doyle, Brian. 'Against the tyranny of the past', *Red Letters*, No. 10, n.d. pp. 23–33

Drakakis, John (ed.). *Alternative Shakespeares*, London, Methuen, 1986

Eagleton, Terry. *Literary Theory: An Introduction*, Oxford, Basil Blackwell, 1983

Eagleton, Terry. 'Capitalism, modernism and postmodernism', *New Left Review*, No. 152, 1985. pp. 60–73

Eagleton, Terry. *William Shakespeare*, Oxford, Basil Blackwell, 1986

Elsom, John (ed.). *Is Shakespeare Still Our Contemporary?* London, Routledge, 1989

Erickson, Peter. *Patriarchal Structures in Shakespeare's Drama*, Berkeley, University of California Press, 1985

Evans, Malcolm. *Signifying Nothing*, Brighton, Harvester, 1986

Felperin, Howard. *The Uses of the Canon: Elizabethan Literature and Contemporary Theory*, Oxford, Clarendon Press, 1990

Ferguson, Margaret, Quilligan, Maureen and Vickers, Nancy J. (eds). *Rewriting the Renaissance: The Discourses of Sexual Differences in Early Modern Europe*, Chicago, University of Chicago Press, 1986

Foucault, Michel. 'What is an author?', in Paul Rabinow (ed.) *The Foucault Reader*, New York, Pantheon, 1984, pp. 118–19

French, Marilyn. *Shakespeare's Division of Experience*, New York, Ballantine Books, 1981

Goldberg, Jonathan. *James I and the Politics of Literature: Jonson, Shakespeare, Donne and their Contemporaries*, Baltimore, Johns Hopkins University Press, 1983

Grady, Hugh. *The Modernist Shakespeare: Critical Texts in a Material World*, Oxford: Clarendon Press, 1991

Grazia, Margreta de. *Shakespeare Verbatim: The Reproduction of Authenticity and the 1790 Apparatus*, Oxford, Clarendon, 1991

Greenblatt, Stephen. *Renaissance Self Fashioning: From More to Shakespeare*, Chicago, University of Chicago Press, 1980

Greenblatt, Stephen. *Forms of Power and the Power of Forms in the Renaissance*, Norman, University of Oklahoma, 1982

Greenblatt, Stephen. *Shakespearean Negotiations: The Circulation of Social Energy in Renaissance England*, Oxford, Clarendon Press, 1988

Hawkes, Terence. *That Shakespeherian Rag: Essays on a Critical Process*, London, Methuen, 1986

Hawkes, Terence (ed.). *Alternative Shakespeares:* Volume 2, London, Routledge, 1996

Hewison, Robert. *In Anger: Culture and the Cold War, 1945–60*, London, Weidenfeld and Nicolson, 1981

Hewison, Robert. *The Culture Industry: Britain in a Climate of Decline*, London, Methuen, 1987

Hodgdon, Barbara. *The End Crowns All: Closure and Contradiction in Shakespeare's History*, Princeton, Princeton University Press, 1991

Holderness, Graham. *Shakespeare's History*, Dublin, Gill and Macmillan, 1985

Holderness, Graham and McCullough, Christopher. 'Boxing the Bard: the cultural politics of television Shakespeare', *Red Letters*, No.18, 1986, pp. 23–33

Holderness, Graham (ed.). *The Shakespeare Myth*, Manchester, Manchester University Press, 1988

Holderness, Graham, Potter, Nick and Turner, John. *Shakespeare: The Play of History*, London, Macmillan, 1988

Holderness, Graham (ed.). *The Politics of Theatre and Drama*, London, Macmillan, 1991

Holderness, Graham, and Loughrey, Bryan. 'Text and stage: Shakespeare, bibliography, and performance studies', in *New Theatre Quarterly*, 9:34, 1993, pp. 187–8

Howard, Jean and O'Connor, Marion F. (eds). *Shakespeare Reproduced: The text in history and ideology*, London, Methuen, 1987

Jardine, Lisa. *Still Harping on Daughters: Women and Drama in the Age of Shakespeare*, Brighton, Harvester, 1983

Jardine, Lisa. *Reading Shakespeare Historically*, London, Routledge, 1996

Joughin, J. (ed.). *Shakespeare and National Culture*, Manchester: Manchester University Press, 1997

Kahn, Coppélia. *Man's Estate: Masculine Identity in Shakespeare*, Berkeley, University of California Press, 1981

Kamps, Ivo (ed.). *Shakespeare Left and Right*, London, Routledge, 1991

Kamps, Ivo (ed.). *Materialist Shakespeare: A History*, London, Verso, 1995

Lenz, Carolyn Ruth, Gayle Green, and Carol Thomas Neely (eds). *The Woman's Part: Feminist Criticism of Shakespeare*, Urbana, University of Illinois Press, 1980

Levin, Richard. 'Bashing the Bourgeois Subject', *Textual Practice* 3, 1989, pp. 76–86

Marcus, Leah. *Puzzling Shakespeare: Local Reading and its Discontents*, Berkeley LA, University of California Press, 1988

Marsden, Jean (ed.) *The Appropriation of Shakespeare: Post-Renaissance Reconstructions of the Works and the Myth*, Hemel Hempstead, Harvester Wheatsheaf, 1991

Masten, Geoffrey. *Textual Intercourse: Collaboration, Authorship and Sexualities in Renaissance Drama*, Cambridge, Cambridge University Press, 1997

Novy, Marianne. 'Demythologizing Shakespeare', *Women's Studies* 9, 1981, pp. 17–27

Novy, Marianne. *Women's Revisions of Shakespeare*, Urbana, University of Illinois Press, 1990

Orgel, Stephen. *The Illusion of Power: Political Theater in the English Renaissance*, Berkeley, University of California Press, 1975

Parker, Patricia, and Hartman, Geoffrey (eds). *Shakespeare and the Question of Theory*, London, Methuen, 1985

Parker, Patricia. *Shakespeare from the Margins: Language, Culture, Contexts*, London and Chicago, University of Chicago Press, 1996

Patterson, Annabel. *Shakespeare and the Popular Voice*, Oxford, Blackwell, 1989

Rabkin, Norman (ed.). *Reinterpretations of Elizabethan Drama*, New York and London, University of Columbia Press, 1969

Rabkin, Norman. *Shakespeare and the Problem of Meaning*, Chicago, University of Chicago Press, 1981

Samuel, Raphael (ed.) *Patriotism: the Making and Unmaking of National Identity*, Vol. 1, *History and Politics*, London, Routledge, 1989

Schwartz, M. and Kahn, Coppélia (eds). *Representing Shakespeare: New Psychoanalytic Essays*, Baltimore, Johns Hopkins University Press, 1980

Shepherd, Simon. *Amazons and Warrior Women: Varieties of Feminism in Seventeenth-Century Drama*, Brighton, Harvester, 1981

Siegel, Paul N. *Shakespeare's English and Roman History Plays: A Marxist Approach*, London, Associated University Presses, 1986

Sinfield, Alan. *Faultlines: Cultural Materialism and the Politics of Dissident Reading*, Oxford, Clarendon Press, 1992

Spinkler, Michael. *Imaginary Relations: Aesthetics and Ideology in the Theory of Historical Materialism*, London, Verso, 1987

Swingewood, Alan. *The Myth of Mass Culture*, London, Macmillan, 1987

Taylor, Gary. *Reinventing Shakespeare: A Cultural History from the Restoration to the Present*, New York, Weidenfeld and Nicholson, 1989

Tennenhouse, Leonard. *Power on Display: The Politics of Shakespeare's Genres*, London, Methuen, 1986

Wayne, Valerie (ed.). *The Matter of Difference: Materialist Feminist Criticism of Shakespeare*, Hemel Hempstead, Harvester Wheatsheaf, 1991

Weimann, Robert. *Shakespeare and the Popular Tradition in Theater: Studies in the Social Dimension of Dramatic Form and Function*, edited by Robert Schwartz, Baltimore, Johns Hopkins University Press, 1987

Williams, Raymond. *Television: Technology and Cultural Form*, London, Fontana, 1974

Williams, Raymond. *Marxism and Literature*, Oxford, Oxford University Press, 1977

DATE DUE
